ENTERTAINING WITH

Also available

The Cranks Recipe Book
The New Cranks Recipe Book
Cranks Light

ENTERTAINING WITH

Cranks

Cranks Restaurants

ORION

An Orion Paperback
First published in Great Britain by J M Dent & Sons Ltd in 1985
This paperback edition published in 1996 by Orion Books Ltd,
Orion House, 5 Upper St Martin's Lane, London WC2H 9EA

Fourth impression 2001

A CIP catalogue record for this book is available from the
British Library.

ISBN 0 75282 579 8

Printed and bound in Great Britain by
The Guernsey Press Co. Ltd, Guernsey,
Channel Islands

Contents

TO ALL THE CRANKS STAFF

who over the past 35 years have worked with us and
contributed so much to our success.

Acknowledgements

We are deeply grateful to the following people without whom this book would not have been possible.

JOHN LAWRENCE trained at the Central School of Art. Twice winner of the Francis Williams Award for illustration, super-vised by the Victoria & Albert Museum, he first began illustrating our brochures and leaflets in 1967 and did the beautiful two-colour wash drawings for *The Cranks Recipe Book*. He has become a close friend and valued colleague. He has illustrated many other books, among them *Watership Down* by Richard Adams, and written several himself includ-ing *George, His Elephant & Castle* and a book of cockney rhyming slang, *Rabbit and Pork*.

DONALD JACKSON MVO won a scholarship to art school in Bolton at the age of 13 years. He later studied at the Central School of Art and Goldsmiths' College and lectured at Camberwell College of Art. He is a leading modern calligra-pher and since 1964 has been Scribe to Her Majesty's Crown Office at the House of Lords. His warm friendship and creative talent have supported us since the inception of Cranks in 1961 and his strong calligraphy and graphics, used throughout our organization and for all our publicity, have contributed so much to the unmistakable style of Cranks.

JANE SUTHERING, the home economist who so skilfully assisted us on the first book, has again advised with these recipes and is responsible for preparing the dishes so beautifully photographed by PAUL WILLIAMS, a true professional and leading expert in food photography; and finally we would like to thank KAREN BOXELL, our tireless secretary for her efficiency and constant help.

Introduction

Since the first edition, in 1985, of *Entertaining with Cranks* many changes have taken place.

In 1985 the Company, in its entirety, was acquired by Guinness Plc. During this period in our history a major principle was changed - our head office moved to Islington and a central bakery and kitchen set up and food was delivered to our London branches from there. It allowed Cranks to open more branches, supply outside catering; then followed meals for British Airways, Virgin Airlines, the THF Welcome Break group and P&O Ferries, and the supply of our bakery products to such famous names as Harrods and Selfridges.

All seemed to be going well when we were sadly sold on again! The company struggled on, badly needing capital for refurbishment and more development. Our loyal long term staff stayed on in spite of events and then in early 1992 we went into the horrors of receivership. This proved a blessing in disguise as our management were able to acquire the company and all the old principles once again were embraced. The current Directors between them have many years of experience in Cranks and total dedication to our early operations. The future looks bright, cooking on the premises is back which brings with it all the delicious smells of freshly baked foods!

Refurbishment of the branches has been completed, a new modern branch has opened in Covent Garden serving a delicious evening menu and all sorts of future plans lie ahead.

Entertaining with Cranks covers a great many different types of occasion - as well as a dinner or drinks party, family celebrations like birthdays or anniversaries, Christmas and Easter, there is the informal lunch or supper party, buffets, picnics and outdoor eating, tea parties and then the times when unexpected guests arrive, or there is a houseful to cope with at weekends. It's all entertaining with a different emphasis. There is something for every occasion amongst these recipes; some of them are very simple and easy to prepare, others more elaborate. We have given preparation and cooking times to help you to plan and many can be prepared in advance or be frozen to use later. All of them follow the basic food principles which we use at Cranks. An important feature of everything we serve is presentation. Choose your dishes for their colour schemes as well as flavour and remember an attractive garnish of fresh herbs or fruit makes all the difference to a savoury dish, just as a sprinkling of toasted nuts or a swirl of cream can improve the looks of a pudding or cake. We have included a short section on finishing touches to suggest ideas.

Over the past 35 years many of the changes we hoped for have come about. There is a fundamental change in food attitudes, real concern about factory farming, additives in food, nutritional values and above all the method by which food is grown and produced. So, looking back, perhaps the motto once found in a Christmas cracker could somehow apply to us - 'A cranks is a little thing which starts a revolution!'

ENTERTAINING WITH

Cranks

List of recipes

Appetizers & Starters

Herbed olives
Spiced mixed nuts
Sesame cheese biscuits
Herbed cheesejacks
Garlic sesame croûtons
Nutties
Avocado & egg mayonnaise
Mushrooms in creamy garlic
& herb sauce
Melon & grapefruit with
ginger & sherry dressing
Mushroom herb pâté
Herb cheese pâté
Fresh asparagus & egg
mousse
Aubergine & tahini dip

Chilli bean dip
Nut & wine pâté
Leek & avocado vinaigrette
Chick pea & tahini dip
Bread tartlets with
mushroom filling
Tzatziki
Tomatoes stuffed with
spinach & pine kernels
Garlic mushrooms
Spicy carrots
Tomatoes stuffed with
guacamole
Ginger cheese ball
Leek & blue cheese soufflé

Soups

Carrot & lemon soup
Curried pea & apple
soup
Cream of celery soup
Fennel soup
Cream of broccoli soup
Cream of spinach & coconut
soup
Spiced lentil soup

Mediterranean vegetable
soup
Cream of pumpkin soup
Courgette & leek soup
Tomato & orange soup
Aduki bean & vegetable
soup
Chinese sweetcorn soup
Sweetcorn chowder

Bean & tomato soup
Minted split pea & tomato
  soup
Chunky tomato broth
Chilled summer soup

Chilled mushroom soup
Iced borscht
Chilled watercress soup
Chilled cucumber &
  yoghourt soup

Salads & dressings

Salad Provençale
Summer salad with blue
  cheese dressing
Bean sprout salad
Cabbage salad
Mixed cress & carrot salad
Oriental salad
Marinated mushrooms
Traditional green salad
Flageolet bean & avocado
  salad
Red kidney bean salad
Bulghur wheat salad
New potato salad
Spinach & pine kernel
  salad
Melon & butter bean salad
Wholewheat salad

Savoury rice salad
Tomato & fresh basil salad
Orange & watercress salad
Seaweed salad
Curried cauliflower &
  French bean salad
Red cabbage in soured
  cream dressing
Mayonnaise
Green herb mayonnaise
French dressing
Spicy salad dressing
Wholegrain mustard
  dressing
Yoghourt dressing with
  aniseed
Lemon dressing
Tofu dressing

Main dishes

Tofu & cashew nuts in sweet
  & sour sauce
Chinese stir-fried vegetables
  with almonds
Aubergine & spinach layer
Curried lentil pie
Mixed vegetables cooked
  with whole spices &
  coconut milk
Spiced lentils
Mushroom & leek pie

Gougère
Spinach & cheese pie
Mixed vegetable risotto
Aubergine Parmesan
Chilli bean & mixed
  vegetable casserole
Russian cabbage pie
Broccoli & cheese roulade
Asparagus & cheese flan
Green lentil rissoles with
  yoghourt sauce

Chilli burgers
Mushroom & herb flan
Leek & dumpling casserole
Baked potatoes stuffed with
  spinach & cheese
Country cheese & onion flan
Baked stuffed marrow
Brazil & cashew nut roast
  with chestnut stuffing &
  red wine sauce
  Brown onion gravy
Baked avocado filled with
  chilli, tomato & cheese

Rice & vegetable bake
Potato & courgette
  fritters
Wholemeal pancakes
Pancakes stuffed with
  ratatouille
Spinach, cheese & tomato
  pancakes
Harvest pancake pie
  White wine sauce
  French onion sauce
  Mushroom sauce
  Lemon & herb sauce

Vegetables

Glazed carrots
Pumpkin
Green beans Italian style
Leeks with cheese &
  watercress sauce
Broccoli with butter &
  flaked almonds
Cabbage with apple &
  juniper berries
Broad beans in creamy herb
  sauce
Courgette & tomato
  ramekins
Spiced cauliflower with
  tomato
Mange-tout with peppers,
  ginger & garlic

Fresh peas with onion &
  lettuce
Spiced okra
Herbed potato bake
Sautéed root vegetables with
  lime
Potatoes boulangère
Viennese red cabbage
Creamed spinach
Steamed carrots with
  caraway
Onions in red wine
Bunches of beans with herb
  butter
Chinese egg fried rice
Spiced savoury rice

Puddings & desserts

Coffee hazelnut meringue
Blackcurrant cheesecake
Carob mousse

Fresh lemon tart
Fresh fruit shortcake
Cranks raw sugar brûlée

Chilled carob charlotte
Continental apple slice
Tropical bananas
Poached peaches with
  summer fruit sauce
Strawberry coconut flan
Baked lemon cheesecake
Pecan pie
Lemon mousse
Poached plums with
  cinnamon cream

Apple & hazelnut lattice
  pie
Winter fruit salad
Fresh fruit salad
Brandied caramel oranges
Fruit mince flan
Strawberry trifle
Rhubarb fool
Apricot & almond crumble
Summer pudding

Bread, rolls & toasts

Wholemeal bread, baps &
  rolls
Cranks crescents
Continental fruit plait
Wholemeal crumpets
Herbed potato bread
Pitta bread
Wholemeal griddle
  cakes
Melba toast

Corn bread
Sesame seed knots
Oatmeal & treacle bread
Indian puris
Paratha – Indian layered
  bread
Savoury scone crescent
Sultana muffins
Blueberry muffins
Potato soda bread

Cakes & biscuits

Coconut fruit mince slice
Carob meringue gâteau
Sponge fingers
Strawberry cream sponge
Victoria sponge
Yoghourt slice
Fudge brownies
Fruit & nut cake
Cranks party cake
Lemon madeira cake
Boiled fruit cake
Carob almond cake
Christmas cake

Honey snaps
Orange wafer biscuits
Carob fruit & nut squares
Honey nut bars
Honey & sesame seed
  squares
Coconut oat bars
Hazelnut fingers
Hazelnut carob biscuits
Muesli biscuits
Coconut oatmeal cookies
Digestive biscuits

Drinks

Pineapple coconut
  crush
White wine cup
Mixed fruit cup
Luaka tea punch
Mulled wine
Cider punch

Cranks homemade
  lemonade
Tomato juice cocktail
Strawberry orange blush
Yoghourt, milk & fruit
  drink
Sparkling fruit drinks

Notes on ingredients

Agar agar. A jelling compound derived from seaweed which produces a cloudy jelly.

Carob. The ground fruit of the carob tree. It can be bought as 75 g bars, or as a powder. Although carob looks and tastes like chocolate, it is rich in vitamins and minerals and contains no refined sugar, caffeine or theobromine.

Cheese. It is possible to buy Cheddar and other hard cheeses prepared with vegetable rennet. This is the type we use at Cranks. There are a variety of low fat soft milk cheeses on the market.

Coconut. Shredded and desiccated coconut are the same thing. Creamed coconut is obtainable from health food shops in 7 oz (198 g) bars. The amount needed can be broken off and melted for use in cooking.

Coffee. Beans, ground and instant coffee can now be bought in decaffeinated form from health food shops. We recommend using this rather than ordinary coffee as it contains no habit-forming caffeine.

Eggs. In this book we have not specified free-range eggs in every recipe but all the eggs we use at Cranks are from free-range hens. The eggs can be easily bought in grocers, supermarkets and health food shops. Be sure to look for the label 'Free Range'.

Flour. We recommend using a 100% wholemeal flour which has been organically grown. At Cranks we use mostly Pimhill flour from the famous Mayall farm in Shropshire, but nowadays it is possible to obtain good organic English flour from health food shops and some supermarkets, as more and more farms are going over to this method of production.

Ginger. Root ginger should be peeled and then grated. Crystallized ginger made with raw sugar is obtainable from most health food shops.

Herbs. Wherever possible use fresh herbs. If using dried herbs remember the flavour is often more concentrated so approximately only half the quantity may be needed.

Margarine. We have given the choice of butter or margarine throughout the recipes. If using margarine be sure it is a polyunsaturated soft vegetable margarine because this contains only 25% saturated fat compared with 61% saturated fat in butter. It is therefore a more healthful alternative.

Oils. Sunflower, safflower and soya oil are all good to use both for cooking and salads; they are mild in flavour and low in saturated fat.

Red kidney beans. These **must be fast-boiled for a minimum of 15 minutes** to destroy a poisonous substance they contain. They should never be sprouted for eating raw.

Salt. At Cranks we use natural sea salt or biochemic salt, a perfectly balanced salt which contains 12 different minerals of which sodium chloride is one. Where salt is measured in the recipes, as in the bread section, we recommend using this type.

Seaweed. Arame sea vegetable is a dried form of edible seaweed available in vacuum-sealed packs from health food shops.

Soya milk. This is obtainable in cartons or powdered form from health food shops. It is produced from soya flour and is therefore suitable for vegans.

Sprouted seeds. Bean sprouts, alfalfa and lentils can be bought ready sprouted, or the seeds can be easily sprouted at home in a jar and are ready to eat in 3–6 days. They are a useful source of vitamins all the year round.

Tofu. This is a soya bean curd with a soft, delicate texture and pale colour. It is sold in slabs or slices and should always be kept refrigerated. The softer consistency is called silken tofu.

Vegetables. Most vegetables need only scrubbing or washing thoroughly, the exceptions to this being onions and garlic that have to be peeled. Keeping the peel retains the fibre and nutrients that lie just beneath the skin. Whenever possible choose organically grown, unsprayed vegetables. These are now available in many health food shops, and even some greengrocers in the country sell them. Best of all grow your own. We recommend steaming all suitable vegetables and saving the water for stock. This is the method we use at Cranks and this way the colour and texture is preserved and overcooking is avoided – there is nothing worse than a soggy vegetable!

Vegetable stock cubes. These are familiar as 'bouillon cubes' and are available with salt or low salt. Another useful standby is vegetable concentrate. There are many different kinds available.

Yeast. If possible always use fresh yeast. It is usually obtainable from bakeries or health food shops. If using dried yeast follow the instructions on the packet. The equivalent proportion is usually half that of fresh yeast.

General notes

Freezing. We have not included instructions for freezing. However, the majority of dishes can be frozen. As a general rule breads and pastry freeze well provided they do not contain cream. There are many good books to refer to on this subject.

Reheating. In many recipes we have mentioned that the dish tastes even better if it is made the day before and reheated, and sometimes it is very useful to be able to cook in advance. When the dish has been cooked it should be allowed to cool at room temperature and then be covered with cling film and put in the fridge. If it can be put in a saucepan reheat by bringing to the boil, adding a little more liquid if necessary, and simmer gently for about 15 minutes. If it is already in an ovenproof dish, put it in a moderate oven 180°C (350°F/Mark 4) covered with foil, for about 30 minutes to heat through. Remove the foil to crisp the top for a final 10 minutes. Never reheat food twice over.

Toasting nuts. For toasting pecans, flaked almonds, coconut, sesame seeds, pine kernels, cashews, sunflower seeds etc. Spread the nuts out on a baking tray and roast in the oven for about 15 minutes at 190°C (375°F/Mark 5) giving them an occasional stir and shake, until browned and crisp.

Labelling. A word of advice when buying ready prepared foods. Do look at the label to see what the ingredients are and avoid ones with lots of additives. The new labelling laws are really in the buyer's favour and are very helpful.

Metrication. The recipes in this book have been written up using a 25 g unit to correspond to 1 oz and 150 ml to ¼ pint. These are approximate recommended conversions. It is therefore important to follow **either** the imperial column **or** the metric column and not to alternate between the two. Always check the weight of a pack before using it. British Standard Institute measure spoons of 1 tsp (5 ml) and 1 tbsp (15 ml) have been used throughout.

Australian equivalents

In Australia the 250 ml measuring cup is used, and the Imperial pint (as in the UK) is 20 fl oz. The Australian tablespoon is larger than the British and holds approximately 20 ml.

US equivalents

In the USA the 8 fl oz measuring cup is used, and the American pint is 16 fl oz. The American tablespoon is smaller than the British and holds approximately 14.2 ml.

US	Imperial	US	Imperial
1 tsp	1 tsp	2 cups	¾ pt
1 tbsp	1 tbsp	(1 pt)	
¼ cup	4 tbsp	2½ cups	1 pt
⅓ cup	5 tbsp	3 cups	1⅕ pts
½ cup	⅕ pt	4 cups	1½ pts
⅔ cup	¼ pt	(1 qt)	
¾ cup	6 oz	6 cups	2½ pts
1 cup	8 oz	(1½ qts)	
1¼ cups	½ pt	8 cups	3¼ pts
1⅓ cups	½ pt	(2 qts)	
1½ cups	12 oz	2½ qts	4 pts
1⅔ cups	13 oz		
1¾ cups	¾ pt		

Wholemeal pastry chart – easy guide to quantities

100% wholemeal flour		Baking powder		Fat (butter and nutter in equal proportions)		Warm water (approx.)	
4 oz	100 g	1 tsp	5 ml	2 oz	50 g	4 tsp	20 ml
5 oz	150 g	1½ tsp	7.5 ml	2½ oz	75 g	2 tbsp	30 ml
6 oz	175 g	1½ tsp	7.5 ml	3 oz	85 g	2–3 tbsp	30–45 ml
7 oz	200 g	2 tsp	10 ml	3½ oz	100 g	3 tbsp	45 ml
9 oz	250 g	2½ tsp	12.5 ml	4½ oz	125 g	3–4 tbsp	45–60 ml
10 oz	300 g	1 tbsp	15 ml	5 oz	150 g	3–4 tbsp	45–60 ml
12 oz	350 g	3 tsp	15 ml	6 oz	175 g	4–5 tbsp	60–75 ml
14 oz	400 g	4 tsp	20 ml	7 oz	200 g	4–5 tbsp	60–75 ml

Put the flour and baking powder into a basin. Rub in the fat until the mixture resembles fine crumbs. Add sufficient warm water to give a soft but manageable dough. Cover with cling film and leave at room temperature until ready to use.

Appetizers & Starters

Herbed olives

Serve these with drinks or pack them into attractive jars to give as presents for your friends. They should be made well in advance to allow the flavours to penetrate.

Black or green olives
Fresh rosemary, thyme & marjoram
Garlic clove, crushed 1
Small dried chilli 1
Olive oil

Preparation time: 10 minutes
No cooking required

Fill a jar with either black or green olives, add a sprig of fresh rosemary, thyme and marjoram, a crushed clove of garlic and a small dried chilli. Cover with olive oil. Seal the jars and leave to marinate for at least a week, and preferably several months.

Don't throw away the oil, keep it to make salad dressings or use again for more olives.

Spiced mixed nuts

Simple to prepare and very tasty. Serve with drinks or as part of a salad selection.

Sunflower seed oil 2 tbsp (30 ml)
Mixed shelled nuts (peanuts, cashew nuts, almonds &
  sunflower seeds) 1 lb (450 g)
Garlic clove, crushed 1
Chilli powder ½ tsp (2.5 ml)
Paprika ½ tsp (2.5 ml)
Soya sauce 2 tbsp (30 ml)

Preparation time: 5 minutes
Cooking time: 10 minutes

Heat the oil in a medium-sized frying pan. Add the nuts and
stir over a low heat for 5–6 minutes, until they begin to turn
a pale golden colour. Add the garlic, chilli and paprika and
continue to stir for a further 2 minutes. Add the soya sauce
and stir to coat the nuts. Fry until all the sauce is used up.
Then remove the pan from the heat. When cold store in an
airtight jar.

Sesame cheese biscuits

Light, crisp biscuits to serve with drinks.

Butter or margarine 4 oz (100 g)
100% wholemeal flour 4 oz (100 g)
Cheddar cheese, grated 4 oz (100 g)
Egg, separated 1
Sesame seeds 2 tbsp (30 ml)
Curry powder 1 tsp (5 ml)
Paprika 1 tsp (5 ml)

Preparation time: 25 minutes + chilling dough 30 minutes
Cooking time: about 10 minutes

Lightly rub the butter into the flour. Then stir in the cheese.
Using a knife, mix in the lightly beaten egg yolk and press

together to make a dough. Try not to handle the mixture too much. Refrigerate for 30 minutes.

Roll out fairly thinly on a lightly floured surface and cut into small rounds – about 2″ (5 cm) in diameter. Brush with lightly beaten egg white and sprinkle with the combined sesame seeds, curry powder and paprika. Bake in the oven at 190°C (375°F/Mark 5) for about 10 minutes, or until golden brown. Cool on a wire tray. Store in an airtight container, or freeze.

Makes 36

Herbed cheesejacks

A savoury variation of Cranks flapjack. These are popular at drinks parties – or as a snack at any time of day.

Millet flakes 1 oz (25 g)
100% wholemeal flour 2 oz (50 g)
Porridge oats 2 oz (50 g)
Cheddar cheese, grated 6 oz (175 g)
Egg, beaten 1
Butter or margarine, melted 2 oz (50 g)
Sage, dried ½ tsp (2.5 ml)
Salt & pepper to taste

Preparation time: 15 minutes
Cooking time: about 40 minutes

Mix all the ingredients together well. Then press into a shallow 7″ (18 cm) square cake tin. Bake in the oven at 180°C (350°F/Mark 4) for about 40 minutes. Cut into thin slices, or bite-size pieces for snacks. Cool on a wire tray. Store in an airtight tin, or freeze.

Makes 12 slices

Garlic sesame croûtons

Serve these with drinks, or add to salads or soups to give an extra crunch.

Egg white 1
Garlic clove, crushed 1
Sesame seeds 2 tsp (10 ml)
Soya sauce 2 tsp (10 ml)
**Day-old wholemeal bread cut in ½" (1 cm) cubes
 3 oz (75 g)**
Oil for frying

Preparation time: 10 minutes
Cooking time: 5 minutes

Whisk together the egg white, garlic, sesame seeds and soya sauce. Quickly dip the bread cubes in the mixture to coat them lightly. Fry in hot oil until crisp and golden. Drain on kitchen paper.

Nutties

Just as they sound – crisp and delicious for a drinks party. These are made from the Brazil & Cashew Nut Roast mixture. Directions are given on pages 123–4.

Avocado & egg mayonnaise

The subtle blend of flavours in this recipe makes it interesting. It can also be served as a main dish.

Mayonnaise (see page 86) ⅓ pint (200 ml)
Natural yoghourt 2 tbsp (30 ml)

Lemon juice 2 tsp (10 ml)
Curry powder ½–1 tsp (2.5–5 ml)
Water 2 tbsp (30 ml)
Parsley, chopped 2 tbsp (30 ml)
Chives, chopped 1 tbsp (15 ml)
Salt & pepper to taste
Eggs, hard-boiled 6
Large avocados 2
Lettuce leaves & parsley sprigs to garnish

Preparation time: 25 minutes
No cooking required

Mix together the mayonnaise, yoghourt, lemon juice, curry powder, water, parsley, chives and salt and pepper. Taste and add a little more curry powder if necessary. Shell and slice the eggs, keeping 6 slices for the garnish. Peel the avocados, remove the stones and chop the flesh. Put the egg and avocado together in a basin and add just enough dressing to coat the slices, stirring carefully. Pile the mixture into a lettuce-lined bowl, or individual dishes, and garnish with parsley sprigs and slices of egg.

Serves 4–6

Mushrooms in creamy garlic & herb sauce

Serve this popular dish with crusty wholemeal rolls to soak up the delicious creamy sauce.

Button mushrooms 1½ lb (675 g)
Butter or margarine 3 oz (75 g)
Garlic cloves, crushed 4
100% wholemeal flour 2 tbsp (30 ml)
White wine 1 fl oz (25 ml)

Vegetable stock cube 1
Salt & pepper to taste
Double cream or soured cream 2 fl oz (50 ml)
Parsley, chopped 2 tbsp (30 ml)
Chives, chopped 1 tbsp (15 ml)

Topping
Wholemeal breadcrumbs, toasted 2 oz (50 g)
Mixed chopped nuts, toasted (*see page 20*) 2 oz (50 g)

Preparation time: 15 minutes
Cooking time: 10 minutes

Wash the mushrooms and pat dry. Melt 2 oz (50 g) of the butter in a pan, add the mushrooms and cook, covered, over a medium heat until just tender. Drain thoroughly and reserve the juices. There should be about ¼ pint (150 ml) of liquid (if necessary add a little vegetable stock to make up this amount). Melt the remaining butter in the pan, add the crushed garlic and cook for a few seconds. Stir in the flour and cook for a few seconds. Then stir in the reserved juices, with the vegetable cube added, white wine and salt and pepper. Stir over the heat until the sauce boils and thickens. Simmer gently for 1 minute. Add the mushrooms and cream and allow to heat through. Stir in the parsley and chives.

Combine the ingredients for the topping and serve the mushrooms in individual ramekins, sprinkled with the toasted breadcrumbs and nuts.

Serves 6

Melon & grapefruit with ginger & sherry dressing

A perfect beginning for a summer dinner party. The dressing can be made in advance and then poured over the prepared melon and grapefruit. For a special occasion, make melon balls instead of slices.

Small melon 1
Grapefruit 2
Small head chicory 1
Grapefruit juice 2 fl oz (50 ml)
Dry sherry 4 tsp (20 ml)
Stem or crystallized ginger, finely chopped 2 tsp (10 ml)
Mustard & cress to garnish

Preparation time: 25 minutes + ½ hour for dressing to stand
No cooking required

Cut the melon in half and scoop out the seeds. Peel and thinly slice. Peel the grapefruit, removing all the white pith, then cut the segments away from the membrane. Trim the base of the chicory and separate the leaves.

Combine the grapefruit juice, sherry and ginger, and leave to stand for at least 30 minutes to allow the flavours to develop.

Arrange 2–3 chicory leaves in the centre of 4 individual dishes. Place the melon and grapefruit slices on either side of the chicory. Garnish with mustard and cress and sprinkle with the ginger and sherry dressing just before serving.

Serves 4

Mushroom herb pâté

This delicious pâté is simple to make and can be prepared the day before it is needed. If the mixture is thinned down by adding a little natural yoghourt it makes an excellent dip.

Large open cap mushrooms 1 lb (450 g)
Butter or margarine 2 oz (50 g)
Thyme, dried ¼ tsp (1.25 ml)

Small bayleaf 1
100% wholemeal flour 3 tbsp (45 ml)
Salt & pepper to taste
Low fat skimmed milk cheese 3 tbsp (45 ml)
Parsley, chopped 3 tbsp (45 ml)
Chives, chopped 3 tbsp (45 ml)
Lemon juice 1 tbsp (15 ml)
Chopped parsley & mushroom slices, soured cream or
   natural yoghourt to garnish

Preparation time: 20 minutes + 1 hour chilling
Cooking time: 5 minutes

Wipe the mushrooms and chop roughly with the skins and
stalks. Melt the butter in a large pan. Add the mushrooms,
thyme and bayleaf and cook until the mushrooms are just
tender. Discard the bayleaf. Stir in the flour, then cook until
the sauce boils and thickens. Simmer for 1 minute to make a
thick sauce, stirring all the time. Season with salt and
pepper. Blend the cooked mushrooms in a liquidizer or food
processor. Leave to cool. Then stir the cheese, parsley and
chives into the mushroom mixture. Add lemon juice to taste
and adjust the seasoning. Refrigerate until ready to serve.
Serve in scoops, garnished with chopped parsley, raw mushroom slices and a little soured cream or natural yoghourt.
Serve with melba toast.

Serves 4–6

Herb cheese pâté

Serve as an appetizer or as an addition to the cheese board at the
end of a meal. Also good for a buffet party.

Low fat skimmed milk cheese 4 oz (100 g)
Cheddar cheese, grated 6 oz (175 g)
Blue-veined cheese, crumbled 2 oz (50 g)

Sherry 2 tsp (10 ml)
French mustard 1 tsp (5 ml)
Black pepper, freshly ground, to taste
Parsley, chopped 2 tbsp (30 ml)
Chives, chopped 1 tbsp (15 ml)
Walnuts, toasted & chopped (*see page 20*) 2 oz (50 g)
Lettuce leaves, olives, parsley & shelled walnut halves to
  garnish

Preparation time: 15 minutes + chilling
No cooking required

Beat all the ingredients together, except the walnuts, until smooth. Shape into a log and wrap in a piece of foil or greaseproof paper. Chill well. Then unwrap and coat with the chopped walnuts. Serve, cut in slices, on a bed of lettuce and garnish with olives, parsley and walnut halves. Serve with melba toast or wholemeal toast.

Serves 8

Fresh asparagus & egg mousse

A delicious starter to make during the short asparagus season. This mousse can be made in advance and will keep in the refrigerator for 1–2 days.

Fresh asparagus 12 oz (350 g)
Agar agar flakes 1 tbsp (15 ml)
Mayonnaise (*see page 86*) 4 tbsp (60 ml)
Parsley, chopped 2 tbsp (30 ml)
Salt & pepper to taste
Cayenne pepper to taste
Eggs, hard-boiled, shelled & mashed 3
Watercress to garnish

Preparation time: 20 minutes
Cooking time: 10 minutes

Trim the stalk ends of the asparagus and steam or cook in boiling water until tender, approximately 10 minutes. Drain, reserving ¼ pint (150 ml) of the cooking liquid. Cut 6 asparagus tips and reserve for the garnish. Put the remainder into a food processor or blender, and blend until puréed. Sprinkle the agar agar over the cool reserved liquid. Bring slowly to the boil. Then simmer gently, whisking all the time, until the agar agar has dissolved – approximately 1 minute. Cool slightly. Add to the asparagus, together with the mayonnaise, parsley, salt, pepper and cayenne, and mix well. When completely cold, fold in the mashed, hard-boiled eggs. Spoon into individual dishes and garnish with the asparagus tips and watercress. Refrigerate until ready to serve. Serve with hot toast or biscuits.

Serves 6

Aubergine & tahini dip

A Middle Eastern dip which can be served as part of a cold table, or with drinks. It will keep in the fridge for several days.

Aubergines 1½ lbs (675 g)
Sunflower or olive oil
Tahini paste 1 tbsp (15 ml)
Garlic clove, crushed 1
Lemon juice 1–2 tbsp (15–30 ml)
Parsley, chopped 6 tbsp (90 ml)
Salt & pepper to taste
Lettuce leaves, parsley & black olives, to garnish

Preparation time: 20 minutes
Cooking time: 45 minutes

Wash the aubergines, remove the stems and cut in half lengthways. Brush the cut sides with oil and place on a baking sheet. Bake in the oven at 180°C (350°F/Mark 4) for approximately 45 minutes, or until the flesh is soft. Cool. Scoop out the flesh, discarding the skins, and put into a blender or food processor. Add the tahini, garlic, lemon juice, parsley and salt and pepper to taste. Beat until smooth. Spoon into a serving dish lined with lettuce leaves and garnish with chopped parsley and black olives. Serve with hot buttered wholemeal toast, pitta bread, melba toast, or raw vegetables for dipping.

Serves 4–6

Chilli bean dip

Hot and spicy, this Mexican-inspired dip is ideal for a winter buffet party. It can be made in advance and reheated when required.

Red kidney beans, soaked overnight 8 oz (225 g)
Soured cream 3 tbsp (45 ml)
Tomato purée 2 tbsp (30 ml)
Garlic cloves, crushed 2
Chilli powder, about ¼ tsp (1.25 ml)
Ground cumin ½ tsp (2.5 ml)
Salt & pepper to taste
Cheddar cheese, grated 2 oz (50 g)
A little soured cream & chopped parsley to garnish

Preparation time: 15 minutes + soaking beans overnight
Cooking time: about 1 hour

Drain the beans. Cover them with fresh water and bring to the boil, *making sure that they boil for at least 15 minutes*. Reduce the heat and simmer until tender, approximately 30 minutes. Drain, reserving about 4 fl oz (100 ml) of the liquid.

Put the beans into a liquidizer goblet or food processor. Add 3 tablespoons (45 ml) of reserved liquid, the soured cream, tomato purée, garlic, chilli powder to taste, cumin, salt and pepper, and blend until smooth. Add a little more liquid if the dip seems too thick. Spoon into a serving dish or individual dishes, top with the cheese and bake in the oven at 180°C (350°F/Mark 4) for 15 minutes or until heated through. Garnish with a little soured cream and chopped parsley. Serve with corn chips.

Serves 4

Nut & wine pâté

This is a variation on the original recipe in our first book. As it's such a favourite we've included it again. It makes an attractive centrepiece for a large dinner party or buffet and should be made at least one day ahead, but it will keep for several days in the refrigerator. Add the glaze on the day of serving.

Butter or margarine 2 oz (50 g)
Small onion, finely chopped 1
Celery sticks, trimmed & finely chopped 3
Garlic clove, crushed 1
Ground cumin ½ tsp (2.5 ml)
Paprika 1 tsp (5 ml)
Fresh basil, chopped 1 tsp (5 ml)
Vegetable stock or water ¼ pt (150 ml)
Red wine ¼ pt (150 ml)
Vegetable stock cube 1
Salt & pepper to taste
Chestnut purée 8 oz (225 g)
Mixed toasted nuts, ground (*see page 20*) 8 oz (225 g)
Wholemeal breadcrumbs 2 oz (50 g)
Parsley, chopped 4 tbsp (60 ml)
Soya sauce 1 tbsp (15 ml)

Eggs, lightly beaten 2
A bunch of black grapes to garnish

Glaze (optional)
Agar agar ¼ pt (150 ml)
Parsley, chopped 1 tbsp (15 ml)
Lemons, sliced & quartered 2

Preparation time: 30 minutes
Cooking time: 40 minutes

Melt the butter in a large pan and cook the finely chopped onion until transparent. Then add the celery and continue to cook for 1 minute. Add the garlic, cumin, paprika, basil, stock, wine, vegetable cube and salt and pepper. Simmer gently for 1 minute. Remove from the heat and stir in the chestnut purée. Then add the nuts, breadcrumbs, parsley, soya sauce and lightly beaten eggs. Mix well.

Spoon the mixture into an 8″ (20 cm) loose-bottomed cake tin which has been lined with greaseproof paper. Bake in the oven at 180°C (350°F/Mark 4) for about 30 minutes until slightly firm to the touch. Leave in the tin until cold, then turn out on to a large plate and chill.

To glaze the top, make up ¼ pint (150 ml) of agar agar following the instructions on the packet. Stir in the chopped parsley and brush half the agar agar mixture over the pâté. Allow to set. Decorate with the lemon slices. Then cover with the remaining agar agar. Refrigerate until ready to serve. Slice and garnish with black grapes on the side. Serve with melba toast or triangles of hot wholemeal toast.

Serves 8–10

Leek & avocado vinaigrette

This starter has an unusual dressing which complements the flavours of the leek and avocado. It can be made in advance and kept in a jar in the fridge.

Large leeks 2
Vegetable stock, about ¼ pt (150 ml)
Large avocado 1
Pine kernels, toasted (*see page 20*) 1 oz (25 g)
Watercress to garnish

Dressing
Red wine vinegar 2 tbsp (30 ml)
Oil 6 tbsp (90 ml)
Tomato purée 2 tsp (10 ml)
Currants 1 oz (25 g)
Small garlic clove, crushed 1
Salt & pepper to taste

Preparation time: 15 minutes
Cooking time: 5 minutes

Trim the leeks and cut them in half lengthways and again crossways. Wash them thoroughly being careful to keep them intact. Place them in a shallow frying pan and pour enough stock to come about halfway up the leeks. Bring to the boil. Then simmer gently, covered, for 5 minutes. Allow to cool in the stock, then drain the leeks and reserve the liquid for soup.

Combine all the dressing ingredients in a screw-top jar and shake well.

Arrange the leeks on 4 plates, fanning them out slightly. Peel, stone and slice the avocado. Place the avocado slices along one side of the leeks. Just before serving, spoon a little dressing over the top. Sprinkle with the pine kernels and garnish with watercress.

Serves 4

Chick pea & tahini dip

Chick peas, soaked overnight 8 oz (225 g)
Lemons, juice of 2

Garlic cloves, crushed 2
Olive oil 5 tbsp (75 ml)
Tahini paste 2 tbsp (30 ml)
Salt & pepper to taste
Water
Paprika & chopped parsley to garnish

Preparation time: 15 minutes + soaking chick peas overnight
Cooking time: 1 hour

Drain the chick peas, then put them into a saucepan and cover with water. Bring to the boil, reduce the heat and cook until tender – about 45–60 minutes. Drain and leave to cool. Put the chick peas into a liquidizer goblet or food processor. Add the lemon juice, garlic, oil, tahini and salt and pepper to taste. Blend until smooth, adding sufficient water to make a thick paste. Check the seasoning and add a little more lemon and garlic if wished. Spoon into a serving dish and sprinkle with paprika and chopped parsley. Serve with hot wholemeal toast or warm pitta bread.

Serves 6–8

Bread tartlets with mushroom filling

These crisp, bread tartlets make a change from pastry, and are much more attractive to look at than mushrooms on toast! The bread cases can be shaped in advance but do not cook them until required.

100% wholemeal bread, 12 thin slices
Butter or margarine 2 oz (50 g)
Small garlic clove, crushed 1

Filling
Butter or margarine 1½ oz (40 g)
Mushrooms, wiped & sliced 1 lb (450 g)

Garlic clove, crushed 1
100% wholemeal flour 2 tbsp (30 ml)
Milk 7 fl oz (200 ml)
Salt & pepper to taste
Spring onions, finely chopped 6
Parsley, chopped 2 tbsp (30 ml)
Double cream or soured cream 2 tbsp (30 ml)

Preparation time: 20 minutes
Cooking time: about 30 minutes

Cut the bread into rounds large enough to fit exactly inside patty tins. Melt the butter and stir in the garlic. Brush both sides of the bread with the garlic butter. Press firmly into the patty tins. Bake in the oven at 190°C (375°F/Mark 5) for 15–20 minutes until golden brown and crisp. Watch them carefully as they will burn very easily.

To make the filling melt the butter in a large saucepan and add the sliced mushrooms. Cook for a few minutes until just tender. Stir in the crushed garlic and flour. Then add the milk. Stir until the mixture boils and thickens. Season with salt and pepper and simmer very gently for 2 minutes, or until the sauce is very thick. Stir in the spring onions, parsley and cream and allow to heat through. Make sure the bread cases are hot (if necessary pop them back in the oven for a minute or two) and spoon the hot filling into each case. Serve immediately.

Serves 6

Tzatziki

This Greek recipe was adapted specially for a Loseley recipe leaflet using their new yoghourt cheese Lebnie – its flavour and texture is ideal. Serve Tzatziki as a starter or as part of a salad selection. It is also delicious served with a spiced savoury main dish. It can be made in advance and refrigerated until required.

Large cucumber 1
Lebnie or low fat skimmed milk cheese 6 oz (145 g) carton
Soured cream ¼ pt (150 ml)
Garlic clove, crushed 1
Fresh mint, chopped 1 tbsp (15 ml)
Parsley, chopped 1 tbsp (15 ml)
Salt & pepper to taste

Preparation time: 15 minutes
No cooking required

Cut a few slices of cucumber for a garnish and put on one side. Coarsely grate the remaining cucumber, put it into a colander and press out as much of the liquid as possible. Beat the Lebnie and soured cream together until smooth. Then add the garlic, herbs and cucumber. Season and mix well. Spoon into a serving dish and garnish with the cucumber slices. Serve with a warm wholemeal bread.

Serves 4

Tomatoes stuffed with spinach & pine kernels

These can be prepared in advance and reheated. They make a very good supper dish.

Medium-sized tomatoes 8
Spinach leaves 4 oz (100 g)
Pine kernels, toasted (*see page 20*) 2 tbsp (30 ml)
Garlic clove, crushed 1
Cheddar cheese, grated 2 oz (50 g)
Brown rice, cooked 2 oz (50 g)
Chopped fresh mixed herbs 1 tbsp (15 ml) or dried mixed herbs 1 tsp (5 ml)
Salt & pepper to taste

Preparation time: 20 minutes
Cooking time: 20–25 minutes

Cut the tops off the tomatoes and remove the seeds. Scoop out the flesh and chop finely together with the tops. Wash the spinach and put it in a saucepan with only the water which clings to the leaves. Cover and cook until tender, then drain and chop finely. Mix together the spinach, pine kernels, garlic, cheese, rice, herbs and the tomato flesh and add salt and pepper to taste. Spoon the mixture into the tomatoes, piling it up slightly at the top. Place in an ovenproof dish and bake in the oven at 180°C (350°F/Mark 4) for 15–20 minutes.

Serves 8 as a starter
*   4 as a main course*

Garlic mushrooms

Ideal for a special dinner party, these stuffed mushrooms are a favourite in our 'Dine and Wine' evening restaurant.

Open cap mushrooms (about 3″ (7.5 cm) in diameter) 8
Butter or margarine 4 oz (100 g)
Garlic cloves, crushed 2
Lemon juice 2 tsp (10 ml)
Parsley, chopped 1 tbsp (15 ml)
Chives, chopped 1 tbsp (15 ml)
Salt & pepper to taste
Wholemeal breadcrumbs 4 oz (100 g)
Parmesan cheese, grated 1 oz (25 g)
Paprika & watercress sprigs to garnish

Preparation time: 20 minutes
Cooking time: 15 minutes

Wipe the mushrooms with a damp cloth. Remove the stalks and chop finely. Mix together the softened butter, garlic, lemon juice, herbs and salt and pepper and beat well. Then beat in the chopped mushroom stalks and the breadcrumbs and divide the mixture evenly between the mushroom caps, pressing it on to each mushroom firmly. Sprinkle with Parmesan cheese. Arrange in a baking dish and bake at 220°C (425°F/Mark 7) for about 15 minutes until sizzling. Sprinkle with paprika, garnish with watercress and serve immediately.

Serves 4

Spicy carrots

Carrots 12 oz (350 g)
Spicy salad dressing (*see page 88*) 1 quantity

Preparation time: 10 minutes
Cooking time: 5 minutes

Scrub the carrots and cut into diagonal slices. Steam, or blanch in boiling water, for 3–5 minutes until slightly tender. Drain and mix with the dressing. Cover and chill. Serve cold as an appetizer or side salad.

Serves 4

Tomatoes stuffed with guacamole

The tomato 'shells' can be prepared in advance. Do not make the guacamole (avocado mixture) too far ahead as it tends to discolour. It is also delicious as a dip – served with crisp biscuits or crudités.

Tomatoes (about 2″ (5 cm) in diameter) 8
Avocados 2
Garlic clove, crushed 1
Lemon juice 1 tbsp (15 ml)

Natural yoghourt 1 tbsp (15 ml)
Green pepper, chopped 1 tbsp (15 ml)
Celery, chopped 1 tbsp (15 ml)
Parsley, chopped 1 tbsp (15 ml)
Cayenne pepper, pinch
Salt & pepper to taste
Watercress or fresh coriander to garnish

Preparation time: 25 minutes
No cooking required

Cut the tops off the tomatoes and using a teaspoon scoop out the flesh and seeds. (Reserve these with the tops for a soup). Turn the tomatoes upside down to drain. Halve, stone, peel and slice the avocados. Reserve quarter of an avocado for garnishing and mash the remainder. Add the garlic, lemon juice, yoghourt, green pepper, celery and parsley. Mix thoroughly and season with cayenne, salt and pepper. Fill the tomatoes with the avocado mixture and garnish the top of each with a tiny slice of avocado and a sprig of watercress or coriander.

Serves 4

Ginger cheese ball

Cottage cheese or low fat soft cheese 8 oz (225 g)
Chopped chives 1 tbsp (15 ml)
Crystallized ginger, finely chopped 2 tbsp (30 ml)
Salt & pepper to taste
Shelled walnuts or pecan nuts, finely chopped 2 oz (50 g)

Preparation time: 15 minutes + several hours chilling
No cooking required

Sieve the cottage cheese, or beat until smooth in a food processor. Add the chopped chives and ginger and season lightly with salt and pepper, mixing well. Refrigerate for several hours until the cheese firms slightly. Shape into a flat round and coat with the finely chopped walnuts or pecan nuts. Serve with melba toast, biscuits or hot wholemeal toast.

Serves 4

Leek & blue cheese soufflé

An impressive starter – make sure your guests are 'at the ready'! The leek mixture and the sauce can be made in advance. Reheat gently, but do not add the egg whites until the last minute. For a main course double the quantities and serve in larger dishes.

Leeks, trimmed & thinly sliced 6 oz (175 g)
Butter or margarine 1 oz (25 g)
Ground nutmeg to taste
Salt & pepper to taste
Soft textured blue cheese, crumbled 2 oz (50 g)
100% wholemeal flour ½ oz (15 g)
Milk 5 fl oz (150 ml)
Cheddar cheese, grated 2 oz (50 g)
Cayenne, pinch
Sage ¼ tsp (1.25 ml)
Parsley, chopped 2 tbsp (30 ml)
Eggs, separated 2

Preparation time: 15 minutes
Cooking time: 25–30 minutes

Wash the leeks thoroughly and drain them well. Melt half the butter in a pan, add the leeks and cook until just tender. Remove from the heat and season with nutmeg, salt and pepper. Stir in the blue cheese and mix well. Divide the mixture evenly between 6 buttered ramekins (each 6 fl oz/ 200 ml).

Melt the remaining butter in a pan, stir in the flour, cook

for a few seconds, then stir in the milk. Continue to stir over the heat until the sauce boils and thickens. Remove from the heat, add the Cheddar cheese, cayenne and sage and season well with salt and pepper. Cool slightly, then add the chopped parsley and egg yolks. Mix thoroughly. Beat the egg whites until stiff peaks form. Using a metal spoon, carefully fold approximately 1 tablespoon of the egg white into the cheese sauce, then fold in the remainder.

Spoon the soufflé mixture over the leeks and bake in the oven at 190°C (375°F/Mark 5) for about 20 minutes or until risen and golden. Serve immediately.

Serves 6

Soups

Carrot & lemon soup

Carrot soup can often be bland, but the addition of lemon gives this extra flavour.

Butter or margarine 1 oz (25 g)
Onion, chopped 1
Potato, chopped 1
Carrots, chopped 1½ lb (675 g)
Garlic clove, crushed 1
Vegetable stock 2 pts (1.2 l)
Vegetable stock cube 1
Salt & pepper to taste
Lemon, grated rind & juice of 1
Chopped chives to garnish

Preparation time: 25 minutes
Cooking time: about 30 minutes

Melt the butter in a large saucepan and add the roughly chopped onion, potato and carrots. Cover the pan and gently cook the vegetables for 5 minutes, stirring occasionally. Stir in the garlic, stock, stock cube and salt and pepper to taste. Cover and cook gently for 20–30 minutes until the vegetables are tender. Blend the soup until smooth in a liquidizer or food processor. Then stir in the finely grated lemon rind and juice and reheat. Serve sprinkled with chopped chives.

Serves 4–6

Curried pea & apple soup

Fresh peas are perfect for this recipe, but when they are not available use dried, allowing 7 oz (200 g), soaked overnight, or frozen peas allowing 14 oz (400 g).

Butter or margarine 1 oz (25 g)
Onion, chopped 1
Curry powder 1 tsp (5 ml)
Vegetable stock 1¼ pts (700 ml)
Vegetable stock cube 1
Fresh green peas, in their pods, 2½ lb (1.125 kg)
Cooking apple, cored & chopped 1
Single cream ¼ pt (150 ml)
Salt & pepper to taste

Preparation time: 20 minutes
Cooking time: about 20 minutes

Melt the butter in a large saucepan and add the onion. Cook gently until transparent. Stir in the curry powder and cook for a minute or two. Then add the stock, stock cube, shelled peas and chopped apple. Cover the pan and simmer gently until the peas are tender, approximately 15 minutes. Blend until smooth in a liquidizer or food processor. Return to the saucepan and stir in the cream. Adjust seasoning to taste. Reheat gently.

Serves 4

Cream of celery soup

Butter or margarine 2 oz (50 g)
Celery, chopped 2 lb (900 g)
Onion, chopped 1
Large potato, chopped 1
Vegetable stock 2 pts (1.2 l)

Vegetable stock cube 1
Salt & pepper to taste
Single cream ¼ pt (150 ml)
Egg yolk 1
Parsley or chives, chopped 2 tbsp (30 ml)

Preparation time: 20 minutes
Cooking time: about 35 minutes

Melt the butter in a large saucepan. Add the chopped celery, onion and potato. Cover and cook gently for 5 minutes, stirring occasionally. Then add the stock, stock cube and salt and pepper to taste. Cover and cook gently for 20–30 minutes until the vegetables are tender. Blend until smooth in a liquidizer or food processor. Return the soup to the pan and allow to heat through. Mix together the cream and the egg yolk. Add a ladle of hot soup to the cream mixture, then pour into the soup. Stir until combined. Reheat but do not allow to boil. Stir in the chopped chives or parsley.

Serves 6

Fennel soup

Butter or margarine 1 oz (25 g)
Medium-sized onion, chopped 1
Large fennel bulb, chopped 10–12 oz (300–350 g)
Medium-sized potato, diced 1
Vegetable stock ¾ pt (450 ml)
Milk ½ pt (300 ml)
Lemon juice 1 tsp (5 ml)
Salt & pepper to taste
Chopped parsley, or fennel, to garnish

Preparation time: 20 minutes
Cooking time: about 45 minutes

Melt the butter in a saucepan and sauté the onion until transparent. Then add the chopped fennel and potato and stir well. Add the stock and bring to the boil. Reduce the heat, cover and simmer gently for about 30 minutes or until the vegetables are tender. Cool, then purée in a food processor or liquidizer goblet. Return the purée to a saucepan and add the milk, lemon juice and salt and pepper to taste. (The consistency of puréed soups is a personal choice – add more vegetable stock if a thinner soup is preferred.) Reheat the soup and sprinkle with chopped herbs.

Serves 4–6

Cream of broccoli soup

Butter or margarine 1 oz (25 g)
Potato, chopped 1
Onion, chopped 1
Broccoli, chopped 1½ lb (675 g)
Garlic clove, crushed 1
Vegetable stock 2 pts (1.2 l)
Salt & pepper to taste
Milk ¼ pt (150 ml)
Chopped chives or parsley to garnish

Preparation time: 20 minutes
Cooking time: 15–20 minutes

Melt the butter in a large saucepan. Add the potato, onion, broccoli and the garlic. Stir to cover with the butter, then add the boiling stock and simmer until the vegetables are just tender, about 15 minutes. Season with salt and pepper. Then blend until smooth in a food processor, or electric blender. Add the milk and carefully reheat. Serve sprinkled with chives or parsley. If a thinner soup is preferred add a little more milk.

Serves 4–6

Cream of spinach & coconut soup

Butter or margarine 1 oz (25 g)
Onion, chopped 1
Potato, chopped 1
Spinach, chopped 1 lb (450 g)
Vegetable stock 1¼ pts (750 ml)
Salt & pepper to taste
Creamed coconut 2 oz (50 g)
Single cream or milk ¼ pt (150 ml)

Preparation time: 25 minutes
Cooking time: 25 minutes

Heat the butter in a large pan. Add the onion and potato and cook gently for 5 minutes, stirring occasionally to prevent sticking. Then add the chopped spinach and stock. Cover and simmer gently for 15 minutes, or until the vegetables are tender. Do not overcook or the spinach will lose its bright green colour. Add the coconut and purée in an electric blender, or food processor. Return the mixture to the pan and stir in the cream or milk. Adjust seasoning to taste and reheat carefully.

Serves 4

Spiced lentil soup

This soup is almost better made the day before as it allows time for the spiced flavour to mellow. It also makes a good main meal, served with wholemeal bread and cheese.

Oil 2 tbsp (30 ml)
Onions, finely chopped 2
Carrots, finely chopped 2
Celery sticks, finely chopped 4
Garlic cloves, crushed 2

Curry powder, to taste, about 1 tbsp (15 ml)
Ground coriander ½ tsp (2.5 ml)
Red lentils 4 oz (100 g)
Vegetable stock 2 pts (1.2 l)
Tomato juice ¼ pt (150 ml)
Salt & pepper to taste
Creamed coconut 1 oz (25 g)
Chopped parsley or fresh coriander to garnish

Preparation time: 20 minutes
Cooking time: about 30 minutes

Heat the oil in a large saucepan. Add the chopped onion, carrots and celery and cook over a low heat for 5 minutes, stirring occasionally to prevent the vegetables from sticking. Stir in the garlic and spices. Cook for a minute or two, then add the lentils, stock and tomato juice. Cover the pan and simmer for about 20 minutes, or until the vegetables are tender. Remove from the heat and stir in the creamed coconut. Adjust seasoning to taste. Serve sprinkled with chopped parsley or coriander.

Serves 4–6

Mediterranean vegetable soup

This tasty and substantial soup makes an excellent supper dish.

Oil 3 tbsp (45 ml)
Onion, chopped 1
Potato, diced 1
Carrots, diced 2
Flageolet or haricot beans, soaked overnight, 4 oz (100 g)
Vegetable stock 2½ pts (1.5 l)
Vegetable stock cube 1
Tomato purée 1 tbsp (15 ml)
Tomatoes, chopped 4

Small wholewheat macaroni 1 oz (25 g)
Fresh green beans, sliced 2 oz (50 g)
Courgette, sliced 1
Salt & pepper to taste
Garlic cloves, crushed 2
Fresh basil, chopped 2 tbsp (30 ml)
Grated cheese to garnish

Preparation time: 30 minutes + soaking beans overnight
Cooking time: about 1 hour

Heat 2 tablespoons of the oil in a large pan. Add the onion, potato and carrots and cook gently for about 5 minutes, stirring occasionally to prevent the vegetables from sticking. Add the drained flageolet beans, stock, vegetable stock cube and tomato purée. Cook gently until the beans and vegetables are almost tender, approximately 40 minutes. Then add the chopped tomatoes, macaroni, green beans and sliced courgette. Season and simmer for a further 10–15 minutes, or until the macaroni is tender. Mix together the crushed garlic and the finely chopped basil, then add the remaining oil to make a thick paste. Just before serving the soup, stir in the basil and garlic mixture. Serve sprinkled with grated cheese.

Serves 6

Cream of pumpkin soup

Our Australian staff introduced us, years ago, to using pumpkins and this soup is an autumn favourite.

Butter or margarine 1 oz (25 g)
Onion, roughly chopped 1
Pumpkin, peeled, seeds removed & chopped 2 lb (900 g)
Potato, chopped 1
Carrot, chopped 1

Vegetable stock 1½ pts (900 ml)
Vegetable stock cube 1
Salt & pepper to taste
Cream, or milk, ¼ pt (150 ml)
Chopped chives to garnish

Preparation time: 25 minutes
Cooking time: about 30 minutes

Melt the butter in a large saucepan and add the vegetables. Cook gently for 5 minutes, stirring occasionally. Do not allow the vegetables to brown. Stir in the stock and stock cube and season to taste. Simmer gently until the vegetables are just tender – about 20 minutes. Then purée in an electric blender or food processor. Return the soup to the pan and stir in the cream. Reheat carefully, and add a little more stock if a thinner soup is preferred. Sprinkle with chives before serving.

Serves 4–6

Courgette & leek soup

Butter or margarine 2 oz (50 g)
Courgettes, sliced 1½ lb (675 g)
Leeks, sliced 8 oz (225 g)
Carrot, sliced 1
Potato, sliced 1
Vegetable stock 1½ pts (900 ml)
Vegetable stock cube 1
Salt & pepper to taste
Single cream 2 fl oz (50 ml)
Parsley, chopped 2 tbsp (30 ml)

Preparation time: 20 minutes
Cooking time: about 25 minutes

Heat the butter in a large saucepan and add the vegetables, stir to coat with butter. Cover the pan and cook over a medium heat for 5 minutes, stirring occasionally. Do not allow them to brown. Add the stock, stock cube and salt and pepper to taste. Bring to the boil, reduce the heat and simmer, covered, for 15–20 minutes until the vegetables are just tender. Blend until smooth in a liquidizer goblet or food processor. Return the soup to the pan and stir in the cream and parsley. Reheat gently without boiling.

Serves 4–6

Tomato & orange soup

An attractively coloured and refreshingly flavoured soup.

Butter or margarine 1 oz (25 g)
Onion, roughly chopped 1
Large carrot, roughly chopped 1
Large potato, roughly chopped 1
Firm ripe tomatoes, chopped 2 lb (900 g)
Vegetable stock 1½ pts (900 ml)
Salt & pepper to taste
Small orange 1

Preparation time: 30 minutes
Cooking time: about 35 minutes

Melt the butter in a large saucepan. Add the onion, carrot and potato and cook gently for 5 minutes, stirring occasionally to prevent the vegetables from sticking. Then add the tomatoes and stock, and salt and pepper to taste. Cover the pan and simmer gently for 20–30 minutes, or until the vegetables are tender. Blend until smooth in a liquidizer or food processor.

Carefully remove the rind from the orange, using a vegetable peeler, being careful not to include the white pith. Cut the rind into thin shreds. Drop them into boiling water and drain immediately. Squeeze the juice from the orange and stir it into the soup. Reheat. Pour into bowls and sprinkle with the orange shreds.

Serves 4–6

Aduki bean & vegetable soup

Aduki beans, soaked overnight, 4 oz (100 g)
Oil 1 tbsp (15 ml)
Onion, finely chopped 1
Garlic clove, crushed 1
Ground cumin, large pinch
Chilli powder, large pinch
Vegetable stock 1½ pts (900 ml)
Vegetable stock cube 1
Tomatoes, finely chopped ½ lb (225 g)
Tomato purée 2 tbsp (30 ml)
Leeks, finely chopped 2
Celery sticks, finely chopped 2
Carrot, finely chopped 1
Salt & pepper to taste
Fresh herbs, chopped 1 tbsp (15 ml) or dried mixed herbs 1 tsp (5 ml)
Parsley, chopped 3 tbsp (45 ml)

Preparation time: 25 minutes + soaking beans overnight
Cooking time: about 1½ hours

Drain the beans. Heat the oil in a large saucepan and fry the onion gently for 1 minute. Stir in the garlic, cumin and chilli powder, mix well and cook for 1 minute. Add the stock, stock cube, tomatoes and the purée, then add the beans and bring to the boil. Cover and simmer gently for about 1 hour, or until almost tender. Add the leeks, celery and carrot to the soup and continue to cook until the vegetables and beans are tender – 20–30 minutes. Season well with salt and pepper and stir in the herbs.

Serves 4

Chinese sweetcorn soup

Fresh corn on the cob is best, but if this is not available use 20 oz (575 g) of frozen corn or two 335 g tins of corn.

Sweetcorn cobs 4
Raw brown sugar, pinch
Oil 2 tbsp (30 ml)
Small onion, finely chopped 1
Garlic cloves, crushed 2
Fresh ginger, grated ½ tsp (2.5 ml)
Vegetable stock 1½ pts (900 ml)
Vegetable stock cube 1
Sesame oil 1 tsp (5 ml)
Soya sauce 1 tsp (5 ml)
Salt & pepper to taste
Arrowroot 1 tbsp (15 ml)
Mushrooms, wiped & thinly sliced 4 oz (100 g)
Spring onions, trimmed & sliced 6
Egg white 1

Preparation time: 25 minutes
Cooking time: 25 minutes

Cook the sweetcorn in boiling water with a pinch of sugar for 10–12 minutes until tender. Cool in the stock. Then using a sharp knife remove the kernels. (Keep the cooking liquid for stock.) Heat the oil in a large saucepan, add the onion and cook until transparent. Then stir in the crushed garlic and ginger. Put the sweetcorn into a food processor or blender and blend until roughly chopped. Add the corn to the onion mixture together with the stock, stock cube, sesame oil, soya sauce and salt and pepper to taste. Bring to the boil and stir in the arrowroot mixed with 2 tablespoons of water. Simmer for 1 minute. Add the mushrooms and spring onions and cook for a further 3 minutes. Then beat together the egg white and 2 tablespoons water. Pour this into the soup in a thin stream, gently stirring all the time. Simmer for 1 more minute, and serve.

Serves 4–6

Sweetcorn chowder

A very popular soup in our 'Dine and Wine' evening restaurant. If fresh corn is not available use 20 oz (575 g) of frozen corn or two 335 g tins of corn.

Large sweetcorn cobs 4
Raw brown sugar, pinch
Butter or margarine 1 oz (25 g)
Leeks, finely chopped 2 or use 1 large onion
Potatoes, diced 1 lb (450 g)
Vegetable stock ¾ pt (450 ml)
Milk 1 pt (600 ml)
Salt & pepper to taste
Chopped parsley to garnish

Preparation time: 25 minutes
Cooking time: about 35 minutes

Cook the sweetcorn in boiling water with a pinch of sugar for 10–12 minutes until tender. Cool in the stock. Then using a sharp knife remove the kernels. (Keep the cooking liquid for stock.) Heat the butter in a pan and add the chopped leeks and potatoes. Cover the pan and cook gently for about 5 minutes, stirring occasionally to prevent sticking. Then add the stock, milk and sweetcorn. Season to taste. Cover and simmer for approximately 15 minutes, or until the vegetables are tender. Serve sprinkled with chopped parsley.

Serves 4–6

Bean & tomato soup

Any dried beans are suitable for this recipe, particularly butter beans or haricot beans.

Dried beans, soaked overnight 8 oz (225 g)
Butter or margarine 1 oz (25 g)
Onions, chopped 2
Garlic cloves, crushed 2
Curry powder 1 tsp (5 ml)
Vegetable stock 2 pts (1.2 l)
Tomato purée 1 tbsp (15 ml)
Vegetable stock cube 1
Firm ripe tomatoes, chopped 1½ lb (675 g)
Salt & pepper to taste
Young spinach leaves, finely chopped 4 oz (100 g)
Parsley, chopped 3 tbsp (45 ml)

Preparation time: 20 minutes + soaking beans overnight
Cooking time: 1¼–1½ hours

Melt the butter in a large pan. Add the chopped onion and cook until transparent. Then add the garlic and curry powder and cook for 1 minute, stirring constantly. Stir in the stock, tomato purée, stock cube and the drained beans. Bring to the boil, reduce the heat, cover and simmer gently for 45 minutes. Add the chopped tomatoes to the soup and continue to cook until the beans are tender, approximately 20–30 minutes. Finally stir in the finely chopped spinach leaves and parsley. Simmer gently for 2 minutes.

Serves 6

Minted split pea & tomato soup

A well flavoured stock is essential for this soup. If necessary use extra vegetable stock concentrate, and for maximum flavour be sure to add the fresh herbs at the end.

Split peas, soaked overnight 4 oz (100 g)
Vegetable stock 2 pts (1.2 l)
Vegetable stock cube 1
Butter or margarine 1 oz (25 g)
Large onion, chopped 1
Tomatoes, chopped 1 lb (450 g)
Freshly chopped mint 3 tbsp (45 ml)
Freshly chopped parsley 1 tbsp (15 ml)
Salt & pepper to taste

Preparation time: 15 minutes + soaking peas overnight
Cooking time: 1½–2 hours

Drain the peas and cover with half the stock. Bring to the boil, reduce the heat, cover and simmer for 1 hour. Melt the butter in a large saucepan, and sauté the chopped onion until golden brown. Add the peas, with their stock, tomatoes and remaining stock. Cover and simmer for up to 1 hour until the peas are tender. Just before serving stir in the fresh herbs and adjust seasoning to taste.

Serves 4–6

Chunky tomato broth

This is a meal in itself, served with a slice of cheese and wholemeal bread. It is important to use a well flavoured stock for this recipe to give a good depth of flavour.

Pot barley 2 oz (50 g)
Butter or margarine 1 oz (25 g)

Medium-sized onion, chopped 1
Garlic clove, crushed 1
White cabbage, finely shredded 4 oz (100 g)
Medium-sized potato, diced 1
Leek, trimmed & sliced 1
Tomatoes, chopped ½ lb (225 g)
Vegetable stock 1 pt (600 ml)
Vegetable stock cube 1
Tomato juice ½ pt (300 ml)
Soya sauce 1 tbsp (15 ml)
Tomato paste 1 tbsp (15 ml)
Thyme, dried ½ tsp (2.5 ml)
Basil, dried ½ tsp (2.5 ml)
Ground bayleaf ¼ tsp (1.25 ml)
Salt & pepper to taste
Chopped parsley to garnish

Preparation time: 25–30 minutes
Cooking time: about 1½ hours

Cover the pot barley with water and boil gently for 1 hour until tender, adding extra water if necessary. Drain. Melt the butter in a large saucepan and sauté the onion and garlic until transparent. Add all the remaining ingredients, except the parsley, and stir in the pot barley. Bring to the boil. Reduce the heat, cover and simmer for 25–30 minutes until all the vegetables are tender. Adjust seasoning to taste and serve sprinkled with parsley.

Serves 4–6

Chilled summer soup

A Cranks variation on Gazpacho – a light, piquant starter. We've used avocado as a garnish, but traditionally this soup is served with a selection of very finely chopped onion, hard-boiled eggs, cucumber, tomato and croûtons.

Tomatoes, roughly chopped 1 lb (450 g)
Cucumber, roughly chopped ½
Spring onions, chopped 3
Small red or green pepper, deseeded & chopped 1
Garlic cloves, crushed 2
Tomato juice ½ pt (300 ml)
Oil 1 tbsp (15 ml)
Wine vinegar 2 tsp (10 ml)
Grated lemon rind ¼ tsp (1.25 ml)
Fresh herbs, chopped (basil, marjoram, mint, chives or
  parsley) 2 tbsp (30 ml)
Salt & pepper to taste
Small avocado 1

Preparation time: 25 minutes + chilling
No cooking required

Put the roughly chopped tomatoes, cucumber, spring onion, pepper and garlic into a blender goblet or food processor and purée. Add the tomato juice, oil, vinegar, lemon rind and herbs and blend until combined. Adjust seasoning to taste and add a little cold water if the soup is too thick. Chill thoroughly.

Just before serving, halve, stone and peel the avocado. Cut 4 thin slices for a garnish and chop the remainder. Stir the chopped avocado into the soup and garnish each bowl with an avocado slice.

Serves 4

Chilled mushroom soup

It's most unusual to have a chilled mushroom soup, but it really is worth trying. This is best made a day ahead to allow the flavours to develop.

Butter or margarine 1 oz (25 g)
Medium-sized potato, diced 1
Large open cap mushrooms, wiped & chopped 1 lb (450 g)
Spring onions, trimmed & sliced 5
Fresh thyme, large sprigs, 2 or dried thyme ¼ tsp (1.25 ml)
Small bayleaf 1
Vegetable stock ¾ pt (450 ml)
Salt & pepper to taste
Single cream ¼ pt (150 ml)
Milk ¼ pt (150 ml)
Parsley, chopped 2 tbsp (30 ml)
Chives, chopped 2 tbsp (30 ml)
Button mushrooms, sliced, 4 to garnish

Preparation time: 20 minutes
Cooking time: about 15 minutes

Melt the butter in a saucepan, add the diced potato and cook for 3 minutes. Add the mushrooms, spring onions, thyme and bayleaf and cook over a medium heat for 2 minutes, stirring once or twice. Add the stock and season with salt and freshly ground pepper. Cover the pan and simmer gently for about 10 minutes until the mushrooms and potato are tender. Cool. Remove the bayleaf and blend the mushroom mixture until smooth. Stir in the cream, milk, chives and parsley. Chill thoroughly. Thin down the soup with a little cold milk if necessary. Serve garnished with slices of raw mushroom.

Serves 4

Iced borscht

Oil 2 tbsp (30 ml)
Medium-sized onion, chopped 1
Raw beetroot, grated 1 lb (450 g)
Small carrot, diced 1
Small potato, diced 1

Vegetable stock 1½ pts (900 ml)
Red wine vinegar or lemon juice 2 tbsp (30 ml)
Tomato purée 1 tbsp (15 ml)
Ground nutmeg ½ tsp (1.25 ml)
Ground bayleaf, generous pinch
Ground cloves, generous pinch
Soured cream or Greek yoghourt ½ pt (300 ml)
Salt & pepper to taste
Chopped chives to garnish

Preparation time: about 30 minutes + chilling
Cooking time: 1¼ hours

Heat the oil in a large saucepan and sauté the onion and
beetroot, stirring occasionally, for 5 minutes. Add the carrot
and potato, stock, vinegar, tomato purée and spices. Bring to
the boil, reduce the heat, cover and simmer for about 1 hour,
until the beetroot is tender. Allow to cool and then purée in a
liquidizer goblet or food processor. Chill. Stir in about
threequarters of the soured cream and adjust seasoning to
taste. To serve ladle the borscht into individual bowls and
garnish with a spoonful of soured cream and sprinkle with
chopped chives.

Serves 6

Chilled watercress soup

Oil 2 tbsp (30 ml)
Medium-sized onion, chopped 1
Watercress, chopped, 2 bunches
Vegetable stock 1 pt (600 ml)
Natural yoghourt ½ pt (300 ml)
Salt & pepper to taste
Watercress leaves to garnish

Preparation time: 25 minutes + chilling
Cooking time: 30 minutes

Heat the oil in a large saucepan and sauté the onion until transparent. Add the watercress and continue cooking for 1–2 minutes, stirring all the time. Add the stock. Bring to the boil, reduce the heat, cover and simmer for about 20 minutes, until the watercress stalks are tender. Allow to cool and then purée in a liquidizer goblet or food processor. Chill. Whisk in the yoghourt and adjust seasoning to taste. Serve garnished with watercress leaves.

Serves 4–6

Chilled cucumber & yoghourt soup

A cool, refreshing soup for a hot summer evening. Best made a day in advance to allow the flavours to mellow.

Large cucumber 1
Tomatoes 1 lb (450 g)
Natural yoghourt 1 pt (600 ml)
Tomato juice ½ pt (300 ml)
Lemon rind, finely chopped 1 tsp (5 ml)
Lemon juice 1 tsp (5 ml)
Salt & freshly ground black pepper to taste
Cayenne pepper, pinch
Paprika ½ tsp (2.5 ml)
Garlic clove, crushed 1
Parsley, chopped 1 tbsp (15 ml)
Chives, chopped 2 tbsp (30 ml)

Preparation time: 10–15 minutes + chilling
No cooking required

Cut some thin slices from the cucumber, allowing 3 per portion, and reserve for garnishing. Chop the remainder.

Combine all the ingredients in a blender goblet or food processor and blend until smooth. Adjust seasoning to taste. Chill thoroughly. Serve garnished with the cucumber slices.

Serves 6

Salads
& Dressings

Salad Provençale

A brightly coloured salad that is ideal for a picnic or barbecue, as it can be packed in a plastic box with a lid and the dressing added just before serving. Carry the dressing separately in a screw-top jar.

Lettuce 1
French beans 8 oz (225 g)
Eggs, hard-boiled & shelled 2
Tomatoes 6
Black olives 2 oz (50 g)
Small onion, sliced 1
Small cauliflower, cut in tiny florets ½
French dressing (*see page 87*)
Chopped parsley to garnish

Preparation time: 30 minutes

Wash and dry the lettuce. Top and tail the beans and drop them into boiling water. Bring back to the boil, drain and rinse well. Chill the lettuce leaves in a salad bowl. Arrange the beans, quartered eggs and tomatoes, olives, onion and cauliflower florets on the lettuce. Serve sprinkled with French dressing and chopped parsley.

Serves 4

Summer salad with blue cheese dressing

This attractive salad makes a good main dish. Different green salad ingredients can be used if you wish, such as endive and watercress.

French beans, topped & tailed 2 oz (50 g)
Broccoli florets 4 oz (100 g)
Young spinach, washed & coarse stems removed
   4 oz (100 g)
Green pepper, deseeded 1
Celery sticks, trimmed 3
Mustard & cress 1 box
Sprouted alfalfa (*see page 19*) 1 oz (25 g)
Avocado 1
Shelled pecan nuts or cashew nuts 2 oz (50 g)

Blue cheese dressing
Blue cheese, crumbled 3 oz (75 g)
Lemon juice 1 tbsp (15 ml)
Garlic clove, crushed 1
Parsley, chopped 2 tbsp (30 ml)
Greek yoghourt or soured cream 5 fl oz (150 ml)
Mayonnaise (*see page 86*) 2 tbsp (30 ml)
Salt & pepper to taste
French dressing (*see page 87*) 2 tbsp (30 ml)

Preparation time: about 30 minutes

Put the beans and the broccoli into boiling water. Bring back to the boil, drain and leave to cool. Shred the spinach finely and slice the green pepper and celery. Halve, stone and peel the avocado and cut it into slices. Put the prepared vegetables into a large salad bowl and stir in the cress, alfalfa and nuts.

To make the dressing blend the cheese, lemon juice, crushed garlic, parsley, yoghourt, mayonnaise, salt and pepper and French dressing together until smooth.

Add the blue cheese dressing to the salad and toss carefully just before serving.

Serves 4

Bean sprout salad

Mung bean sprouts or lentil sprouts (*see page 19*)
   8 oz (225 g)
Red pepper deseeded & sliced 1
Cheddar cheese, grated 3 oz (75 g)
Chives, chopped 2 tbsp (30 ml)
Parsley, chopped 2 tbsp (30 ml)
Cherry tomatoes & parsley sprigs to garnish

Dressing
Ripe tomatoes, chopped 8 oz (225 g)
Lemon juice 2 tsp (10 ml)
Garlic clove, crushed 1
Oil 2 tbsp (30 ml)
Salt & freshly milled pepper to taste

Preparation time: 20 minutes

Mix all the salad ingredients together in a bowl.

To make the dressing put the chopped tomatoes, lemon juice, garlic, oil and seasoning into a liquidizer goblet or food processor and blend until puréed. Just before serving spoon on enough dressing to coat the salad and toss well. Garnish with cherry tomatoes and sprigs of parsley.

Serves 4

Cabbage salad

Small Dutch white cabbage ½
Red cabbage 2 oz (50 g)
Mustard & cress 1 box
Yoghourt dressing (*see page 89*) to taste

Preparation time: 15 minutes

Using a sharp, serrated knife, cut across the grain of the cabbages to produce tiny shreds. Place in a salad bowl with the mustard and cress and toss in yoghourt dressing.

Serves 4

Mixed cress & carrot salad

Watercress 2 bunches
Mustard & cress 2 boxes
Medium-sized carrots, grated 4
Lemon dressing (*see page 89*) to taste

Preparation time: 25 minutes

Wash and dry the watercress, removing any coarse stalks. Put it in a bowl with the mustard and cress and grated carrot. Just before serving add sufficient lemon dressing to coat the leaves and toss well.

Serves 4

Oriental salad

The combination of colour and shapes makes this an attractive salad for a buffet. Take care to cut the salad vegetables exactly as described.

Large red pepper, deseeded 1
Carrot, trimmed 1
Spring onions, trimmed 4
Celery sticks, trimmed 3
Mushrooms, wiped 4 oz (100 g)
Bean sprouts 3 oz (75 g)
Sesame seeds, toasted (*see page 20*) 1 tbsp (15 ml)

Dressing
Oil 2 fl oz (50 ml)
Sesame oil 1 fl oz (25 ml)
Soya sauce 1 tbsp (15 ml)
Lemon juice 1 tbsp (15 ml)
Garlic clove, crushed 1
Crystallized ginger, chopped ½ tsp
Salt & pepper to taste

Preparation time: 20 minutes

Cut the pepper and the carrot into very thin strips. Diagonally slice the spring onions and celery. Slice the mushrooms. Put these ingredients in a bowl together with the bean sprouts.

To make the dressing put the oils, soya sauce, lemon juice, crushed garlic, ginger, salt and pepper into a screw-topped jar and shake until combined, or blend in a liquidizer.

Add enough dressing to the salad to coat the sliced vegetables, and mix well. Sprinkle with the toasted sesame seeds and serve at once.

Serves 4–6

Marinated mushrooms

If this can be made a day in advance the flavour will be even better!

Firm white mushrooms 1 lb (450 g)
Chives, chopped 2 tbsp (30 ml)
Parsley, chopped 2 tbsp (30 ml)
Garlic clove, crushed 1
Salt & pepper to taste
French dressing (*see page 87*) to taste

Preparation time: 15 minutes + 1½ hours chilling

Wipe the mushrooms with damp kitchen paper and slice them. Put the mushrooms, herbs and crushed garlic into a bowl. Season with salt and pepper. Then add enough French dressing to coat the mushrooms and toss well. Refrigerate for at least an hour before serving.

Serves 4

Traditional green salad

This is an excellent side salad to have with a main course. To vary it, use an equal quantity of finely shredded, young spinach, curly endive or other green leafy salad vegetable instead of the lettuce.

Medium-sized lettuce 1
Spring onions, trimmed 4
Watercress 1 bunch
Cucumber ½
Fresh herbs, chopped (parsley, chives, basil, mint)
  2 tbsp (30 ml)
French dressing (*see page 87*) to taste

Preparation time: 20 minutes

Wash, dry and shred the lettuce. Finely chop the spring onions. Wash the watercress thoroughly, removing any tough stalks, and chop roughly. Slice the cucumber. Mix the salad ingredients together in a large bowl. Just before serving add enough French dressing to coat the salad. Toss well.

Serves 4–6

Flageolet bean & avocado salad

A sophisticated salad we serve in our 'Dine and Wine' evening restaurant.

Flageolet or haricot beans, soaked overnight 8 oz (225 g)
Young spinach, washed & coarse stems removed
   2 oz (50 g)
Spring onions, trimmed 4
Avocado 1

Herb dressing
Wine vinegar 2 tbsp (30 ml)
Oil 6 tbsp (90 ml)
Garlic clove, crushed 1
French mustard ¼ tsp (1.25 ml)
Fresh herbs, chopped (basil, mint, chives, parsley, thyme)
   2 tbsp (30 ml)
Salt & pepper to taste

Preparation time: 20 minutes + soaking beans overnight
Cooking time: about 40 minutes

Drain the beans. Cover with boiling water and cook until tender – about 40 minutes. Drain well and leave to cool. Finely slice the spinach and chop the spring onions. Halve, stone, peel and slice the avocado. Lightly mix the beans, spinach, spring onions and avocado together in a bowl.

Shake all the dressing ingredients together in a screw-top jar and add to the salad just before serving. Toss well.

Serves 6

Red kidney bean salad

Red kidney beans, soaked overnight ¾ lb (350 g)
Tomatoes, finely chopped 1 lb (450 g)
Spring onions, trimmed & chopped 6
Parsley, chopped 3 tbsp (45 ml)
Ripe avocado to garnish 1

Dressing
Wine vinegar 3 tbsp (45 ml)
Oil 9 tbsp (135 ml)
Garlic cloves, crushed 2
Salt & pepper to taste
Ground cumin, large pinch
Chilli powder, large pinch

Preparation time: 30 minutes + soaking beans overnight
Cooking time: about 45 minutes

Drain the beans. Cover with fresh water and bring them to the boil *and boil rapidly for 15 minutes*. Reduce the heat and simmer until the beans are tender – about 30 minutes. Drain well. Put them in a bowl and add the dressing to the beans while they are still warm.

To make the dressing put all the ingredients into a screwtop jar and shake well.

Leave the beans to cool and then add the finely chopped tomatoes, spring onions and parsley and mix lightly. Spoon into a serving dish. Halve, stone and peel the avocado. Cut into slices and use to garnish the salad.

Serves 8

Bulghur wheat salad

A colourful and 'different' salad for a party, that is best made a day in advance. Be sure to use the best quality dried apricots for this recipe.

Bulghur wheat 8 oz (225 g)
Dried apricots, washed & sliced 6 oz (175 g)
Fresh mint, chopped 4 tbsp (60 ml)
Parsley, chopped 2 oz (50 g)
Spring onions, trimmed & sliced 6
Garlic cloves, crushed 2
Lemon juice 4 tbsp (60 ml)
Oil 3 tbsp (45 ml)
Salt & pepper to taste
Fresh mint or parsley sprigs to garnish

Preparation time: 20 minutes

Cover the bulghur wheat with boiling water and leave to stand for 15 minutes until the water is absorbed.

Combine the wheat, sliced apricots, mint, parsley, spring onions, garlic, lemon juice, oil and salt and pepper to taste. Mix well. Garnish with fresh herbs just before serving.

Serves 6–8

New potato salad

For this ever popular salad try to select potatoes which are all the same size so that they cook evenly.

Small new potatoes 2 lb (900 g)
French dressing (*see page 87*) 3 tbsp (45 ml)
Mayonnaise (*see page 86*) ¼ pt (150 ml)
Caraway seeds (optional) 1 tsp (5 ml)
Salt & pepper to taste
Chives, chopped 2 tbsp (30 ml)

Preparation time: 20 minutes
Cooking time: about 20 minutes

Scrub the potatoes and steam or boil them until just tender –
about 20 minutes. Cool. Combine the French dressing and
the mayonnaise. Put the potatoes into a bowl and add the
dressing and the caraway seeds. Mix well. Season to taste and
sprinkle with chopped chives.

Serves 6

Spinach & pine kernel salad

Young spinach, washed & coarse stalks removed
   8 oz (225 g)
Tomatoes 1 lb (450 g)
Radishes, trimmed 6
Spring onions, trimmed 4
Parsley, chopped 3 tbsp (45 ml)
Pine kernels, or broken cashews, toasted (*see page 20*)
   2 oz (50 g)

Dressing
Wine vinegar 1 tbsp (15 ml)
Oil 4 tbsp (60 ml)
Garlic clove, crushed 1
Salt & pepper to taste
French mustard ½ tsp (2.5 ml)

Preparation time: 25–30 minutes

These salad ingredients need to be very finely chopped. Shred
the spinach. Finely chop the tomatoes and thinly slice the
radishes and spring onions. Just before serving the salad, add
the parsley and nuts and mix all the ingredients together in a
bowl.

   To make the dressing put the vinegar, oil, crushed garlic,
salt, pepper and mustard in a screw-top jar and shake until
combined. Pour over the salad and toss well.

Serves 4–6

Melon & butter bean salad

This is a very unusual salad and a good choice for a main course in the summer

Butter beans, soaked overnight 4 oz (100 g)
Shelled walnuts, roughly chopped 2 oz (50 g)
Celery sticks, trimmed & sliced 3
Medium-sized cantaloup melon or ogen melon, deseeded,
   peeled & chopped 1
Melon slices, celery leaves & walnut halves to garnish

Dressing
Mayonnaise (*see page 86*) ¼ pt (150 ml)
Lemon juice 2 tsp (10 ml)
French dressing (*see page 87*) 1 tbsp (15 ml)
Curry powder ½ tsp (2.5 ml)
Salt & pepper to taste

Preparation time: 30 minutes + soaking beans overnight
Cooking time: about 45 minutes

Drain the beans. Cover with fresh water, bring to the boil and cook until tender – about 45 minutes. Drain and cool. Mix the butter beans, chopped walnuts, celery and chopped melon together.

   Put all the dressing ingredients into a small bowl and stir until combined. Just before serving, spoon on enough dressing to coat the salad, and toss lightly. Garnish with melon slices, celery leaves and walnut halves.

Serves 4

Wholewheat salad

This salad is a meal in itself! Try to buy organically grown wholewheat berries. They are usually obtainable in health food shops.

Wholewheat berries, soaked overnight 8 oz (225 g)
Red pepper, deseeded 1
Spring onions, trimmed 6
Peanuts, roasted (*see page 20*) 2 oz (50 g)
Parsley, chopped 2 tbsp (30 ml)
Salt & pepper to taste
Mayonnaise (*see page 86*) ¼ pt (150 ml)

Preparation time: 15–20 minutes + soaking berries overnight
Cooking time: 30–40 minutes

Drain the wheat. Cover with boiling water and cook until just tender – 30–40 minutes depending on taste. Drain and leave to cool. Finely chop the red pepper and slice the spring onions. Add the rest of the ingredients and mix well. Adjust the seasoning. Cover and refrigerate until required.

Serves 4–6

Savoury rice salad

This is an ideal rice salad for a buffet. It can be prepared a day in advance. To make it a main dish add chopped or grated cheese, chopped nuts or freshly grated raw vegetables before serving.

Long grain brown rice 8 oz (225 g)
Medium-sized onions 2
Oil 4 tbsp (60 ml)
Soya sauce 2 tbsp (30 ml)
Salt & pepper to taste
Parsley, chopped 4 tbsp (60 ml)

Preparation time: 15 minutes
Cooking time: 30–40 minutes

Cook the rice in boiling water for 30–40 minutes until just tender. (Half way through the cooking time start cooking the onions.) Slice the onions thinly. Heat the oil in a frying pan and sauté the onions until pale golden. Drain the rice and add to the onions in the frying pan. Stir in the soya sauce and adjust the seasoning.

Sprinkle with parsley and stir through lightly. Allow to cool.

Serves 4

Tomato & fresh basil salad

There is nothing to compare with the flavour of fresh basil. If it is unobtainable, use fresh mint or coriander instead.

Firm ripe tomatoes 1 lb (450 g)
Large ripe avocado 1
Fresh basil, chopped 3 tbsp (45 ml)
Salt & freshly milled black pepper to taste
French dressing (*see page 87*) to taste

Preparation time: 20 minutes

Slice the tomatoes. Halve, stone, peel and slice the avocado. Arrange the tomato and avocado on a serving plate and sprinkle with the chopped fresh basil. Season to taste. Spoon a little French dressing over the salad and serve at once.

Serves 4

Orange & watercress salad

This is a most refreshing and colourful summer salad, and a good side salad. Grapefruit can be used instead of orange.

Large oranges 4
Watercress 2 bunches
French dressing (*see page 87*) 2 tbsp (30 ml)
Grated orange rind 1 tsp (5 ml)
Fresh mint, chopped 1 tbsp (15 ml)

Preparation time: 30 minutes

Using a serrated knife, peel the oranges, removing all the white pith, and cut away the segments. Do this holding the orange over a plate to catch the juice. Wash the watercress, remove any coarse stems and chop roughly. Arrange the orange segments and the watercress on a serving plate. Mix together the French dressing, orange rind, chopped mint and reserved orange juice and spoon over the orange and watercress. Serve at once.

Serves 4–6

Seaweed salad

Arame sea vegetable (*see page 18*) ½ oz (15 g)
Small onion 1
Cucumber ½
Small lettuce 1
Wine or cider vinegar 2 tbsp (30 ml)
Sesame oil 3 tbsp (45 ml)
Soya sauce 3 tbsp (45 ml)

Preparation time: 25 minutes

Soak the seaweed in boiling water for 5 minutes. Drain. Cover with cold water, leave for 10 minutes and then drain it thoroughly. Cut the onion into very fine rings. Thinly slice the cucumber and shred the lettuce. Put all the salad ingredients into a bowl. Stir the vinegar, sesame oil and soya sauce together, spoon over the salad and serve at once.

Serves 4

Curried cauliflower & French bean salad

Large cauliflower 1
French beans 4 oz (100 g)
Parsley, chopped 3 tbsp (45 ml)
Lettuce leaves & toasted coconut (*see page 20*) **to garnish**

Dressing
Soured cream 3 fl oz (75 ml)
Mayonnaise (*see page 86*) **3 fl oz (75 ml)**
French dressing (*see page 87*) **3 fl oz (75 ml)**
Curry powder 1 tsp (5 ml)
Salt & pepper to taste

Preparation time: 30 minutes
Cooking time: 10 minutes

Cut the cauliflower into small florets. Drop them into boiling water. Bring back to the boil quickly. Then remove from the heat and drain. Rinse in cold water. Drain. Top and tail the beans, cut them in half and blanch them in the same way as the cauliflower.

Stir all the dressing ingredients together until well combined. Put the cauliflower, beans and parsley into a bowl and add enough dressing to coat the vegetables. Mix lightly. Put the salad into a serving dish lined with lettuce leaves and serve sprinkled with toasted coconut.

Serves 4–6

Red cabbage in soured cream dressing

This salad goes well with Baked Potatoes Stuffed with Spinach & Cheese or Leek & Dumpling Casserole.

Small red cabbage ½
Sultanas 2 oz (50 g)

Parsley, chopped 2 tbsp (30 ml)
Sunflower seeds, toasted (*see page 20*) 2 tbsp (30 ml)
Lettuce leaves & mustard & cress to garnish

Dressing
Soured cream ¼ pt (150 ml)
Wine vinegar 1 tbsp (15 ml)
Garlic clove, crushed 1
Salt & pepper to taste
Freshly grated horseradish to taste

Preparation time: 20 minutes

Finely shred the cabbage and mix with the sultanas, parsley
and sunflower seeds. Stir all the dressing ingredients together
in a small bowl and then add enough to coat the salad. Mix
well. Spoon into a serving dish lined with lettuce leaves and
garnish with mustard and cress.

Serves 4–6

Mayonnaise

Egg 1
Salt ½ tsp (2.5 ml)
French mustard ½ tsp (2.5 ml)
Cider or wine vinegar 2 tsp (10 ml)
Oil ½ pt (300 ml)

Preparation time: 10–20 minutes

Break the egg into a liquidizer goblet. Add the salt, mustard
and vinegar. Blend for 10 seconds. While the liquidizer is
switched on, slowly feed in the oil through the lid. As the oil
is added the mayonnaise will become thick.

To make the mayonnaise by hand, beat the egg, salt,
mustard and vinegar together in a basin using a wooden

spoon or balloon whisk. Then add the oil, *drop by drop*, until half the oil has been used. Continue adding in very small quantities until all the oil has been incorporated.

Makes ½ pint (300 ml)

Green herb mayonnaise

The fresh herbs used in this can be varied.

Mayonnaise (*see page 86*) ½ pt (300 ml)
Freshly chopped parsley 2 tbsp (30 ml)
Freshly chopped chives 1 tbsp (15 ml)
Freshly chopped mint 1 tbsp (15 ml)

Mix all the ingredients together in a small bowl.

French dressing

This is Cranks' standard version of French dressing used through-out our restaurants. To make a thinner dressing add a little water. Store in the refrigerator.

Lemons, juice of 2
Cider or wine vinegar 4 tbsp (60 ml)
Salt 1½ tsp (7.5 ml)
Pepper ½ tsp (2.5 ml)
French mustard 1 tbsp (15 ml)
Raw brown sugar (optional) 2 tsp (10 ml)
Oil ¾ pt (450 ml)

Put the lemon juice, vinegar, salt, pepper, mustard and sugar into a jug. Whisk with a fork until evenly blended, then slowly work in the oil.

or

Put all the ingredients together in a liquidizer goblet and blend for a few seconds.

or

Shake all the ingredients together in a screw-top jar.

Makes about 1 pt (600 ml)

Spicy salad dressing

Fresh green chilli, deseeded & finely chopped 1
Garlic clove, crushed 1
Raw brown sugar 1 tsp (5 ml)
Curry powder ¼ tsp (1.25 ml) or a pinch of chilli powder
Oil 4 tbsp (60 ml)
Lemon juice 2 tbsp (30 ml)
Freshly chopped coriander or parsley 2 tbsp (30 ml)
Salt & pepper to taste

Shake all the ingredients together in a screw-top jar, or whisk together in a small bowl.

Wholegrain mustard dressing

Oil 6 tbsp (90 ml)
Wine or cider vinegar 2 tbsp (30 ml)
Clear honey 1 tbsp (15 ml)
Wholegrain mustard 1 tbsp (15 ml)
Fresh tarragon, chopped 1 tbsp (15 ml) or dried tarragon
   1 tsp (5 ml)
Salt & pepper to taste

Shake all the ingredients together in a screw-top jar, or whisk together in a bowl.

Yoghourt dressing with aniseed

Natural yoghourt ¼ pt (150 ml)
Parsley, chopped 2 tbsp (30 ml)
Aniseed 1 tsp (5 ml)
Raw brown sugar ½ tsp (2.5 ml)
Salt & pepper to taste

Stir all the ingredients together in a small bowl. If wished thin the dressing with a little unsweetened fruit juice, milk or water.

Alternative
This dressing can be varied with celery seed ½ tsp (2.5 ml), fennel or caraway 1 tsp (5 ml) instead of aniseed.

Lemon dressing

Lemon juice 2 tbsp (30 ml)
Oil 2 tbsp (30 ml)
Water 2 tbsp (30 ml)
Raw brown sugar 2 tsp (10 ml)
Salt & pepper to taste
Fresh herbs, chopped (optional) 1 tbsp (15 ml)

Shake all the ingredients together in a screw-top jar, or whisk together in a bowl.

Tofu dressing

Silken tofu 5 oz (150 g)
Wholegrain mustard 2–3 tsp (10–15 ml)
Lemon juice 1 tbsp (15 ml)
Spring onions, chopped 3
Salt & pepper to taste

Purée all the ingredients in a liquidizer goblet.

Main Dishes

Tofu & cashew nuts in sweet & sour sauce

Chinese-style cooking is ideal for vegetables as they keep their bright colours and crispness. The preparations can all be done beforehand – but cook at the last minute.

Tofu 10½ oz (297 g)
Oil 3 tbsp (45 ml)
Cashew nuts 2 oz (50 g)
Mange-tout peas or green beans, topped & tailed
   3 oz (75 g)
Spring onions, trimmed 4
Celery sticks, trimmed 3
Red pepper, deseeded 1
Mushrooms, wiped 4 oz (100 g)
Small green chilli, finely chopped 1
Garlic cloves, crushed 2
Green ginger, grated 1 tsp (5 ml)
Soya sauce 1 tbsp (15 ml)
Wine vinegar 1 tsp (5 ml)
Pineapple juice 4 tbsp (60 ml)
Brown sugar 1 tbsp (15 ml)
Water 6 tbsp (90 ml)
Tomato purée 1 tsp (5 ml)
Sesame oil 1 tsp (5 ml)
Arrowroot 2 tsp (10 ml)
Bean shoots 3 oz (75 g)
Salt & pepper to taste

Preparation time: 30 minutes
Cooking time: 10 minutes

Cut the tofu into 1" (2.5 cm) cubes and place on several layers of kitchen paper to drain thoroughly. Heat the oil in a large frying pan or wok, add the cashew nuts and cook until light golden in colour. Remove with a slotted spoon and drain. Add the tofu to the oil and carefully cook until lightly browned. Remove from the pan.

Prepare the vegetables. If the mange-tout are large cut them in half. Diagonally slice the spring onions and celery. Thinly slice the red pepper and slice the mushrooms. Add all these to the pan and toss over a high heat for 1 minute. Then add the finely chopped chilli, crushed garlic and ginger. Mix the soya sauce, vinegar, pineapple juice, sugar, water, tomato purée, sesame oil and arrowroot together in a bowl and add to the vegetables. Toss over the heat until the sauce thickens and coats the vegetables. Then stir in the bean shoots, tofu and nuts. Allow to heat through. Adjust the seasoning to taste and serve immediately with boiled brown rice.

Serves 3–4

Chinese stir-fried vegetables with almonds

A very attractive dish which can be cooked extremely quickly. All the vegetables may be prepared in advance.

Oil 2 tbsp (30 ml)
Whole blanched almonds 2 oz (50 g)
Celery sticks, trimmed 2
Spring onions, trimmed 4
Cauliflower florets 4 oz (100 g)
Red pepper, deseeded 1
Button mushrooms, wiped 4 oz (100 g)

Mange-tout peas 4 oz (100 g)
Fresh ginger, grated 1 tsp (5 ml)
Garlic cloves, crushed 2
Vegetable stock 9 fl oz (275 ml)
Sesame oil 2 tsp (10 ml)
Soya sauce 2 tbsp (30 ml)
Dry sherry 2 tsp (10 ml)
Arrowroot 2 tsp (10 ml)
Bean shoots 4 oz (100 g)
Salt & pepper to taste

Preparation time: 30 minutes
Cooking time: 7–8 minutes

Heat the oil in a frying pan or wok, add the almonds and cook gently until golden. Remove from the pan using a slotted spoon and drain. Prepare the vegetables, cutting the celery and spring onions diagonally into thin slices. Blanch the cauliflower florets by dropping them into boiling water. Return to the boil and cook for 1 minute. Drain. Then rinse them under cold water. Cut the red pepper into thin strips and slice the mushrooms. Top and tail the mange-tout. Return the pan to the heat, add the celery and cook for 1 minute. Then add the red pepper, spring onion, mange-tout, mushrooms, ginger and crushed garlic. Stir-fry the vegetables over the heat until just tender. Then add the combined vegetable stock, sesame oil, soya sauce, sherry and arrowroot. Continue to toss the vegetables until the liquid boils and thickens to give a glossy sauce. Then add the cauliflower, bean shoots and almonds. Season to taste, and heat through quickly. The vegetables must not be overcooked. Serve immediately. Egg fried rice (*See page 154*) goes well with this.

Serves 3–4

Aubergine & spinach layer

A delicious layered dish which can be made completely in advance, then heated through when required. Pasta and spinach layer can be made in the same way, using 3–4 sheets lasagne per serving instead of the aubergine.

Aubergines 1½ lb (675 g)
100% wholemeal flour to coat
Oil 4 tbsp (60 ml)
Butter or margarine 1 oz (25 g)
Spinach, well washed & chopped 1½ lb (675 g)
Cheddar cheese, grated 2 oz (50 g)

Tomato nut sauce
Oil 3 tbsp (45 ml)
Onion, chopped 1
Garlic cloves, crushed 2
100% wholemeal flour 2 tbsp (30 ml)
Tomatoes 1½ lb (675 g)
Tomato purée 2 tbsp (30 ml)
Vegetable stock cube 1
Yeast extract 2 tsp (10 ml)
Basil, dried ½ tsp (2.5 ml)
Oregano, dried ½ tsp (2.5 ml)
Salt & pepper to taste
Red or green pepper, deseeded & sliced 1
Mushrooms, wiped & sliced 6 oz (175 g)
Chopped mixed nuts, toasted (*see page 20*) 4 oz (100 g)

Cheese topping
Butter or margarine 2 oz (50 g)
Small onion, chopped 1
100% wholemeal flour 3 tbsp (45 ml)
Milk ¾ pt (450 ml)
Ground nutmeg ¼ tsp (1.25 ml)
Cayenne pepper, pinch
Salt & pepper to taste

Cheddar cheese, grated 4 oz (100 g)
Eggs, lightly beaten 2

Preparation time: 1 hour
Cooking time: about 1 hour

Remove the stalks and cut the aubergines in half lengthways. Place on a greased oven tray and bake at 220°C (425°F/ Mark 7) for 10–15 minutes. Cool. Carefully peel the aubergines (the skins should peel away easily now) and cut them lengthways into ½″ (1 cm) slices. Coat with flour. Heat the oil in a large frying pan, then add the butter. Cook the aubergine slices until golden on both sides. Drain well on kitchen paper. Put the spinach into a saucepan with only the water which clings to the leaves. Cover and cook until tender. Put a layer of aubergine into the base of a large oven proof dish. Cover with half the tomato nut sauce. Put half the spinach into the dish to cover the sauce. Repeat these layers with the remaining aubergine, sauce and spinach. Cover with the cheese topping and sprinkle with the grated cheese. Bake in the oven at 190°C (375°F/Mark 5) for 30–40 minutes until golden.

Tomato nut sauce
Purée the whole tomatoes in a food processor or blender. Heat the oil in a pan, add the chopped onion and cook until transparent. Stir in the crushed garlic and continue to cook for a second. Stir in the flour. Then add the puréed tomatoes and the stock cube, yeast extract, herbs, tomato purée, and salt and pepper. Stir over the heat until the sauce boils and thickens. Simmer for 1 minute. Add the sliced pepper and simmer for 1 minute. Then add the mushrooms and continue to cook until the vegetables are tender. Remove from the heat and stir in the nuts.

Cheese topping
Melt the butter in a pan, add the chopped onion and cook until transparent. Stir in the flour and cook for 1 minute.

Add the milk, nutmeg, cayenne and salt and pepper. Stir until the sauce boils and thickens. Simmer gently for 1 minute. Remove from the heat, stir in the cheese and allow it to melt. Cool. Then stir in the lightly beaten eggs.

Serves 6

Curried lentil pie

This can be prepared in advance and is ideal for a family party – or make it up in individual pies for a picnic.

Wholemeal shortcrust pastry made with 12 oz (350 g) of 100% wholemeal flour (*see page 22*)
Beaten egg to glaze

Filling
Oil 2 tbsp (30 ml)
Large onion, chopped 1
Garlic cloves, crushed 2
Curry powder, 1 tbsp (15 ml)
Ground coriander 1 tsp (5 ml)
Ground cumin 1 tsp (5 ml)
Green lentils 12 oz (350 g)
Water 1¼ pts (700 ml)
Tomato purée 4 tbsp (60 ml)
Vegetable stock cube 1
Small green pepper, deseeded & sliced 1
Small leek, trimmed & sliced 1
Celery sticks, trimmed & sliced 2
Salt & pepper to taste

Preparation time: 35 minutes
Cooking time: 1½–1¾ hours

Heat the oil in a saucepan and fry the chopped onion until transparent. Add the garlic, curry powder, coriander and cumin and cook for a few seconds. Then stir in the lentils, water, tomato purée and vegetable stock cube. Cover the pan and simmer gently for 30 minutes. Add the sliced pepper, leek and celery and mix together well. Continue to cook for approximately 20–30 minutes, keeping the pan covered, until the lentils and vegetables are tender. It may be necessary to add a little more water. The filling should be moist but not too wet. Adjust the seasoning to taste and leave the filling to cool.

Roll out half the pastry to line a 9″ (23 cm) pie plate. Put the lentil filling into the pastry case and brush the rim with water. Roll out the remaining pastry to cover the pie. Seal and trim the edges. Cut a small hole in the top of the pie with a sharp knife. Decorate with left-over trimmings and brush with beaten egg to give a good glaze to the pie. Bake in the oven at 200°C (400°F/Mark 6) for 30–40 minutes until golden brown. Delicious served with chutney and sliced banana.

Serves 8

Mixed vegetables cooked with whole spices & coconut milk

If possible make this dish a day ahead so the flavour has time to develop. Coconut adds a delicate creaminess to the vegetables.

Boiling water 1¼ pts (700 ml)
Desiccated coconut 8 oz (225 g)
Oil 3 tbsp (45 ml)
Large onion, chopped 1
Garlic cloves, crushed 2
Ground cumin 2 tsp (10 ml)
Coriander seeds, crushed 1 tsp (5 ml)
Cardamom pods, crushed 8
100% wholemeal flour 2 tbsp (30 ml)

Vegetable stock cube 1
Sultanas 2 oz (50 g)
Salt & pepper to taste
Mixed vegetables:
  Carrot, diced 1
  Potato, diced 1
  Celery sticks, trimmed 5
  Small cauliflower, cut into florets ½
  Mushrooms, wiped & sliced 4 oz (100 g)
  Red pepper, deseeded & sliced 1

Preparation time: 30 minutes
Cooking time: about 30 minutes

Pour the boiling water over the coconut, mix, and leave to cool. Then strain off the liquid pressing as much liquid out of the coconut as you can, using your hands. Discard the coconut. Heat the oil in a pan, add the chopped onion and cook until transparent. Add the crushed garlic and the spices and cook for 1–2 minutes. Stir in the flour, then add the coconut milk, stock, cube, sultanas and salt and pepper to taste. Stir over the heat until the sauce boils and thickens. Then add the carrot, potato and celery, cover and cook for 10–15 minutes until almost tender. Add the cauliflower florets and cook for 5 minutes. Finally add the sliced mushrooms and pepper. Cover the pan and continue to cook until all the vegetables are tender – about 5 minutes.

We suggest serving this with boiled rice, chutney and sliced banana, topped with toasted coconut.

Serves 4–6

Spiced lentils

This can be made up to 24 hours in advance which gives time for the flavours to mellow. Try topping the hot lentils with creamy mashed potato and then brown under the grill.

Oil 2 tbsp (30 ml)
Large onion, chopped 1
Garlic cloves, crushed 2
Curry powder 1 tbsp (15 ml)
Ground cumin 2 tsp (10 ml)
Ground coriander 1 tsp (5 ml)
Green lentils 12 oz (350 g)
Water 1½ pts (900 ml)
Vegetable stock cube 1
Tomato purée 3 tbsp (45 ml)
Celery sticks, trimmed & sliced 3
Leek, trimmed & sliced 1
Tomatoes, chopped 3
Salt & pepper to taste
Sliced tomato & parsley sprigs to garnish

Preparation time: 20 minutes
Cooking time: about 1¼ hours

Heat the oil in a saucepan, add the chopped onion and cook until transparent. Add the crushed garlic and spices and stir over the heat for 1–2 minutes. Stir in the lentils and coat them with the spices. Then add the water, stock cube and tomato purée. Bring to the boil and simmer gently, covered, for 30 minutes. Add the celery, leek and chopped tomato. Cover and continue to simmer for a further 30 minutes, or until the lentils are tender. Stir the mixture occasionally throughout the cooking period to prevent sticking and add a little more water if the lentils become too dry. Adjust seasoning to taste. Garnish with chopped tomato and parsley.

Serves 4–6

Mushroom & leek pie

The flavours of mushroom and leek together make a particularly delicious filling for this pie.

**Wholemeal shortcrust pastry using 12 oz (350 g) of 100%
wholemeal flour (*see page 22*)**
Beaten egg to glaze

Filling
Butter or margarine 2½ oz (60 g)
Leeks, trimmed & sliced 1½ lb (675 g)
Open cap mushrooms, wiped & sliced 1 lb (450 g)
100% wholemeal flour 4 tsp (20 ml)
Vegetable stock cube 1
Garlic cloves, crushed 2
Ground nutmeg to taste
Salt & pepper to taste
Parsley, chopped 4 tbsp (60 g)
Low fat skimmed milk cheese 7 oz (200 g)
Eggs, lightly beaten 2

Preparation time: about 35 minutes
Cooking time: 30–40 minutes

Melt 2 oz (50 g) of the butter in a pan, add the sliced leeks
and cook gently until tender. Remove the leeks from the
pan, reserving the buttery juices. Add the sliced mushrooms
and cook until tender, stirring occasionally. Drain the mushrooms and add them to the leeks. Put the reserved juices in a
measuring jug, and if necessary make up to ¼ pint (150 ml)
with stock. Melt the remaining butter in a small saucepan,
stir in the flour, and cook for a minute, stirring. Add the
reserved liquid, stock cube, garlic, nutmeg, salt and pepper
to taste. Stir over the heat until the sauce boils and thickens.
Simmer gently for a few minutes to give a thick sauce.
Combine the mushrooms, leeks and sauce and then stir in the
parsley, cheese and lightly beaten eggs. Taste to make sure
the mixture is well seasoned. Cool.

Roll out half the pastry and line a 9" (23 cm) pie plate. Put
the cold mushroom and leek mixture into the pastry case and
brush the edges with beaten egg. Roll out the remaining
pastry to cover the pie. Seal and trim the edges. Cut a small
hole in the top of the pie with a sharp knife. Decorate with

the left-over pastry trimmings and brush with lightly beaten egg. Bake in the oven at 200°C (400°F/Mark 6) for 30–40 minutes or until golden.

Serves 8

Gougère

A stunning dinner party dish or an attractive alternative to the traditional nut roast for a special occasion.

Choux pastry
Butter or margarine 2 oz (40 g)
Water ¼ pt (150 ml)
100% wholemeal flour 3 oz (75 g)
Baking powder 1 tsp (5 ml)
Eggs, lightly beaten 2
Cheddar cheese, grated 3 oz (75 g)
Cayenne pepper, pinch
French mustard 1 tsp (5 ml)
Salt, pinch
Beaten egg to glaze
Chopped parsley to garnish

Filling for gougère
Butter or margarine 2 oz (50 g)
Small onion, finely chopped 1
Open cap mushrooms, wiped & sliced 1 lb (450 g)
Thyme, pinch
Garlic cloves, crushed 2
100% wholemeal flour 2 tbsp (30 ml)
Vegetable stock ¼ pt (150 ml)
Vegetable stock cube 1
Tomato purée 1 tbsp (15 ml)
Paprika 1 tsp (5 ml)
Salt & pepper to taste
Red pepper, deseeded & diced 1

Courgette, trimmed & sliced 1
Leek, trimmed & sliced 1
Soured cream 2 tbsp (30 ml)

Preparation time: 30 minutes
Cooking time: 1 hour

Put the butter and water into a saucepan. Stir over the heat until the butter has melted. Bring to the boil, remove from the heat and stir in the flour and baking powder. Beat with a wooden spoon until the mixture forms a ball and leaves the sides of the pan clean. Cool slightly. Gradually beat in the beaten eggs. Then add two-thirds of the cheese and the cayenne, mustard and salt. Mix together well. Place teaspoonfuls of the mixture, almost touching, around the edge of a greased, shallow, ovenproof serving dish, about 8″ (20 cm) in diameter. Brush the choux pastry lightly with beaten egg, then sprinkle with the remaining cheese. Bake in the oven at 220°C (425°F/Mark 7) for approximately 30 minutes until golden and puffy.

Remove from the oven and fill the centre of the dish with the hot filling. Serve sprinkled with chopped parsley.

Filling

Melt the butter in a pan and cook the finely chopped onion until transparent. Then add the sliced mushrooms and cook until just tender. Add the thyme and garlic, cook for a few seconds, then stir in the flour. Add the stock, stock cube, tomato purée, paprika, and salt and pepper to taste. Stir until the sauce boils and thickens. Simmer gently, uncovered, for 5 minutes. Then add the chopped pepper, courgette and leek and continue to cook until the vegetables are just tender – about 10 minutes. Stir in the soured cream.

Serves 4

Spinach & cheese pie

This pie is a meal in itself – perfect for picnics.

**Wholemeal shortcrust pastry made with 12 oz (350 g) of
wholemeal flour (*see page 22*)**
Beaten egg to glaze

Filling
Spinach, well washed & shredded 2 lb (900 g)
Butter or margarine 1 oz (25 g)
Large onion, chopped 1
Garlic cloves, crushed 2
Cheddar cheese, grated 3 oz (75 g)
Soured cream 4 fl oz (100 ml)
Parsley, chopped 2 tbsp (30 ml)
Eggs, lightly beaten 3
Grated nutmeg ¼ tsp (1.25 ml)
Salt & pepper to taste

Preparation time: 45 minutes
Cooking time: 50–60 minutes

Put the washed and shredded spinach in a saucepan with
only the water which clings to the leaves and place over a
medium heat until it is just cooked and no free liquid remains.
Stir once or twice to prevent it sticking and to help it cook
evenly. Melt the butter in a small pan, add the chopped
onion and cook until transparent. Combine the spinach,
onion, garlic, cheese, soured cream, parsley, lightly beaten
eggs, nutmeg and seasoning.

Roll out half the pastry to fit a 9″ (23 cm) pie dish. Put the
spinach filling into the pastry case. Brush the rim with beaten
egg. Roll out the remaining pastry to cover the pie, trim the
edges. Make a hole in the centre with a sharp knife. Decorate
the top of the pie with the trimmings and glaze with beaten
egg. Bake in the oven at 200°C (400°F/Mark 6) for 30–40
minutes until golden. Serve hot or cold.

Serves 8

Mixed vegetable risotto

Sauce
Butter or margarine 2 oz (50 g)
Onion, chopped 1
Thyme, dried ½ tsp (2.5 ml)
Tarragon, dried ½ tsp (2.5 ml)
Garlic cloves, crushed 2
100% wholemeal flour 2 tbsp (30 ml)
Ripe tomatoes 1 lb (450 g)
Water 4 fl oz (100 ml)
White wine 2 fl oz (50 ml)
Vegetable stock cube 1
Yeast extract 2 tsp (10 ml)
Tomato purée 2 tbsp (30 ml)
Raw brown sugar 1 tsp (5 ml)
Salt & pepper to taste
Red pepper, deseeded & diced 1
Green pepper, deseeded & diced 1
Mushrooms, wiped & sliced 4 oz (100g)
Sultanas 1 oz (25 g)
Cashew nuts, toasted (*see page 20*) 1 oz (25 g)

Risotto
Long grain brown rice 8 oz (225 g)
Carrot, trimmed & diced 1
Celery sticks, trimmed & diced 2
Cauliflower florets 4 oz (100 g)
Courgette, sliced 1
Leek, trimmed & sliced 1
Cheddar cheese, grated 3 oz (75 g)
Sliced red pepper & parsley sprigs to garnish

Preparation time: 45 minutes
Cooking time: about 1 hour

Melt the butter in a large saucepan, add the chopped onion and cook until transparent. Add the thyme, tarragon and garlic and cook for a few seconds. Stir in the flour. Then add the tomatoes which have been finely chopped, preferably in a blender or food processor. Add the water, wine, stock cube, yeast extract, tomato purée, sugar and salt and pepper. Stir over the heat until the sauce boils and thickens. Add the chopped red and green peppers and simmer gently, covered, for 1 minute. Add the mushrooms and sultanas and continue to cook for another minute. Stir in the nuts. The sauce should be rich and full of flavour.

Cook the rice in boiling water until tender – about 30 minutes. Drain. Steam, or sauté, the carrot, celery, courgette and leek until they are just tender – about 15–20 minutes. (These vegetables may be varied according to season.)

Combine the rice, vegetables and sauce and spoon into an ovenproof dish. Sprinkle with the grated cheese, and bake in the oven at 190°C (375°F/Mark 5) for about 20 minutes until heated through. Garnish with red pepper and parsley.

Serves 6

Aubergine Parmesan

A rich and substantial dish which can be made completely in advance and reheated when required. Serve with a crisp green salad.

Medium-sized aubergines 2
100% wholemeal flour to coat
Oil 6 tbsp (90 ml)
Butter or margarine 1 oz (25 g)
Cheddar cheese, grated 4 oz (100 g)
Parmesan cheese, grated 1 tbsp (15 ml)
Mozarella or Emmenthal cheese, sliced 4 oz (100 g)
Watercress to garnish

Tomato sauce
Oil 2 tbsp (30 ml)

Onions, chopped 2
Garlic cloves, crushed 3
Fresh ripe tomatoes, finely chopped 2 lb (900 g)
Tomato purée 1 tbsp (15 ml)
Vegetable stock cube 1
Basil, dried 1 tsp (5 ml)
Oregano, dried ½ tsp (2.5 ml)
Parsley, chopped 4 tbsp (60 ml)
Salt & pepper to taste

Preparation time: 30 minutes
Cooking time: about 50 minutes

This method of preparing the aubergines helps prevent them from absorbing too much oil. Remove the stalks and cut the aubergines in half lengthwise. Place on a greased oven tray and bake in the oven at 220°C (425°F/Mark 7) for 10–15 minutes. Cool. Then carefully peel the aubergines (the skins should come away quite easily now) and cut into ½″ (1 cm) slices. Coat with flour. Heat the oil in a large frying pan, then add the butter. Cook the aubergine slices until golden on both sides. Drain well on kitchen paper. Arrange half the aubergine slices in an ovenproof dish. Spoon over half the tomato sauce. Then half the mixed cheeses. Repeat the layers. Bake in the oven at 200°C (400°F/Mark 6) for 20–30 minutes until heated through. Serve garnished with watercress.

Tomato sauce
Heat the oil in a saucepan, add the chopped onion and cook until transparent. Then stir in the garlic. Finely chop the tomatoes in a food processor or blender. Then put them in a pan with the onion, tomato purée, stock cube, basil and oregano. Simmer gently, stirring occasionally, for about 15 minutes or until the sauce is thick. Stir in the parsley and adjust seasoning to taste.

Serves 4–6

Chilli bean & mixed vegetable casserole

Ideal for a winter weekend – it can be made in advance for Sunday lunch. Serve with baked potatoes or boiled rice.

Red kidney beans, soaked overnight 6 oz (175 g)
Oil 2 tbsp (30 ml)
Onion, chopped 1
Garlic cloves, crushed 2
Ground cumin 1 tsp (5 ml)
Chilli powder ¼–½ tsp (1.25–2.5 ml)
100% wholemeal flour 2 tbsp (30 ml)
Ripe tomatoes 2 lb (900 g)
Tomato purée 2 tbsp (30 ml)
Vegetable stock cube 1
Yeast extract 2 tsp (10 ml)
Raw brown sugar 1 tsp (5 ml)
Salt & pepper to taste
Small carrot, diced 1
Small potato, diced 1
Celery sticks, trimmed & diced 2
Cauliflower florets 4 oz (100 g)
Red or green pepper, deseeded & sliced 1
Mushrooms, wiped & sliced 4 oz (100 g)
Courgette, trimmed & sliced 1
A little grated Cheddar cheese, soured cream or natural yoghourt, avocado slices & chopped parsley to garnish

Preparation time: 30 minutes + soaking beans overnight
Cooking time: 1–1¼ hours

Drain the beans. Then cook them in plenty of water until tender – about 1 hour, *making sure the beans boil rapidly for at least 15 minutes*. Drain. Heat the oil in a large saucepan, add the chopped onion and cook until transparent. Add the crushed garlic, cumin and chilli and cook for a further minute. Stir in the flour, then add the tomatoes which have been finely chopped, preferably in a blender or food processor. Add the tomato purée, stock cube, yeast extract, sugar, salt and pepper. Simmer gently for 5 minutes. The sauce should be quite thick and rich in flavour. Add the carrot and potato to the sauce, cover the pan, and continue to simmer for approximately 10 minutes until the carrot is almost cooked. Then add the celery, cauliflower and pepper and simmer for five minutes. Finally, add the sliced mushrooms and courgette and continue to cook, covered, until all the vegetables are tender – 5–10 minutes. Stir in the beans and allow to heat through. Serve topped with grated cheese, soured cream, chopped parsley and slices of avocado.

Serves 4–6

Russian cabbage pie

This is an impressive pie for a party. Serve it with a tomato salad and a bowl of soured cream.

Yeast dough
Fresh yeast 1 oz (25 g)
Raw brown sugar 1 tbsp (15 ml)
100% wholemeal flour 1 lb (450 g)
Milk ½ pt (300 ml)
Butter or margarine 4 oz (100 g)
Salt 1 tsp (5 ml)
Egg yolk 1
Beaten egg to glaze

Filling
Green cabbage 1 lb (450 g)
Butter or margarine 2 oz (50 g)
Spring onions, trimmed & sliced 6
Mushrooms, wiped & sliced 3 oz (75 g)
Eggs, hard-boiled & shelled 2
Raw brown sugar 1 tsp (5 ml)

Parsley, chopped 3 tbsp (45 ml)
Salt & pepper to taste

Preparation time: 30—40 minutes + 1¼ hours rising time for
  dough
Cooking time: 40 minutes

Yeast dough

Mix the yeast and half the sugar in a small bowl until dissolved. Sprinkle with 1 teaspoon of the flour and leave in a warm place. Put the milk, butter, salt and remaining sugar into a pan and heat until lukewarm. Put the remaining flour into a basin, make a well in the centre and pour in the milk mixture, yeast and lightly beaten egg yolk. Stir with a wooden spoon, gradually incorporating the flour. Work the dough with one hand until smooth and elastic. This takes about 3 minutes. Cover with polythene and leave to prove in a warm place for 1 hour until it has doubled in size.

Knead the dough lightly on a floured board. Then cut it in half. Roll out one half to form a 10″ (25 cm) round and put it on a greased baking tray. Brush the edge with beaten egg. Spoon the prepared filling on to the dough to within ½″ (1 cm) of the edge. Roll out the remaining dough to cover the pie. Brush the edges with beaten egg or water and press together firmly. Cover with polythene and leave to prove in a warm place for 15 minutes. Then brush the top with beaten egg and bake in the oven at 200°C (400°F/Mark 6) for 30—40 minutes or until golden. Tap the crust with your knuckles and if it sounds hollow it will be cooked.

Filling

Remove the outer leaves and core from the cabbage and shred finely. Heat the butter in a large frying pan and stir in the cabbage. Cook for 5 minutes. Then add the spring onions and mushrooms. Continue to cook for a further 5 minutes until the vegetables are almost tender. Stir from time to time to prevent them from sticking. Remove from the heat and cool slightly. Stir in the chopped hard-boiled eggs, sugar, parsley, and the salt and pepper to taste and mix well.

Serves 6–8

Broccoli & cheese roulade

This unusual dish is light and delicate in flavour. Like a soufflé it should be eaten at once. Make the filling first.

Filling
Small broccoli florets 4 oz (100 g)
Butter or margarine ½ oz (15 g)
100% wholemeal flour 1 tbsp (15 ml)
Milk 4 fl oz (100 ml)
Spring onions, trimmed & finely chopped 3
Cheddar cheese, grated 3 oz (75 g)
Watercress to garnish

Soufflé mixture
Eggs, separated 4
Fresh herbs, chopped (parsley, chives, thyme, marjoram, basil) 4 tbsp (60 ml)
Double cream 2 tbsp (30 ml)
Salt & pepper to taste
Parmesan cheese, grated

Preparation time: 25 minutes
Cooking time: about 15 minutes

Steam or cook the broccoli in boiling salted water until tender – about 5–7 minutes, and drain. Melt the butter in a saucepan, stir in the flour and cook for a minute, stirring. Stir in the milk and the spring onions and cook gently until the sauce boils and thickens. Simmer very gently for 2 minutes. Season with salt and pepper and then stir in the grated cheese. Add the broccoli and keep warm while preparing the roulade.

Mix together the egg yolks, herbs and cream and season well with salt and pepper. Beat the egg whites until stiff and fold into the egg yolk mixture using a metal spoon. Pour the mixture into a 10″ × 8″ (25 cm × 20 cm) tin lined with greased, greaseproof paper or silicone paper. Bake in the oven at 200°C (400°F/Mark 6) for about 10 minutes or until light golden and firm to the touch.

Sprinkle a light coating of Parmesan cheese on to a sheet of greaseproof paper and unmould the soufflé mixture on to it. Carefully remove the lining paper and spread the warm filling to within 1″ (2.5 cm) of the edges. Roll up carefully, starting at a short end, and serve at once cut in slices.

Serves 4

Asparagus & cheese flan

Tiny broccoli or cauliflower florets can be used when asparagus is not in season.

Wholemeal shortcrust pastry made with 5 oz (150 g) of
flour (*see page 22*)
Fresh asparagus, peeled & ends trimmed 8 oz (225 g)
Parsley, chopped 3 tbsp (45 ml)
Chives, chopped 1 tbsp (15 ml)
Cayenne pepper, pinch
Salt & pepper to taste
Cheddar cheese, grated 4 oz (100 g)
Eggs 3
Single cream 8 fl oz (250 ml)

Preparation time: 20 minutes
Cooking time: 40–50 minutes

Roll out the pastry on a lightly floured surface and use to line an 8″ (20 cm) fluted flan tin. Bake 'blind' in the oven at 200°C (400°F/Mark 6) for 10 minutes. Cool. Gently steam or cook the asparagus in boiling water until just tender, approximately 5–10 minutes depending on the thickness of the stalks. Cut into 1" (2.5 cm) pieces, leaving the tips about 2" (5 cm) long. Arrange the asparagus evenly over the pastry base and sprinkle with the herbs, cayenne, salt, pepper and grated cheese. Whisk the eggs and cream together and pour carefully over the asparagus. Bake in the oven at 190°C (375°F/Mark 5) for 30–40 minutes until the filling has set and is golden brown.

Serves 4–6

Green lentil rissoles with yoghourt sauce

Lentils absorb the flavour of spices very well and are ideal for making savoury rissoles. Yoghourt sauce is a sharp, refreshing contrast to the spiced flavour. These rissoles can be made up in advance and kept in the fridge until ready to be fried.

Green lentils 8 oz (225 g)
Hot water 1 pt (600 ml)
Butter or margarine 2 oz (50 g)
Onion, finely chopped 1
Carrot, finely chopped 1
Green pepper, deseeded & finely chopped 1
Garlic cloves, crushed 2
Cayenne pepper ¼ tsp (1.25 ml)
Ground coriander ½ tsp (2.5 ml)
Ground cumin ½ tsp (2.5 ml)
Curry powder ½ tsp (2.5 ml)
Tomato purée 2 tsp (10 ml)
Salt & pepper to taste
Parsley, chopped 1 tbsp (15 ml)

Coating
100% wholemeal flour 2 oz (50 g)
Eggs, lightly beaten 2

Wholemeal breadcrumbs 2 oz (50 g)
Porridge oats 2 oz (50 g)
Oil for shallow frying

Yoghourt sauce
Plain natural yoghourt ½ pt (300 ml)
Parsley, chopped 2 tbsp (30 ml)
Chives, chopped 1 tbsp (15 ml)
Garlic clove, crushed 1
Ground cumin ¼ tsp (1.25 ml)
Lemon juice to taste
Salt & pepper to taste

Preparation time: 30 minutes
Cooking time: about 1 hour

Put the lentils and hot water into a pan. Bring to the boil, reduce the heat and then simmer gently, covered, for about 30 minutes or until the lentils are tender and all the liquid is absorbed. Stir occasionally while they are cooking and add more water if necessary.

Heat the butter in a large pan, add the onion and cook for a minute or two. Then add the carrot and pepper and continue to cook until tender – 5–10 minutes. (The vegetables need to be very finely chopped and this is best done in a food processor). Add the spices, tomato purée and salt and pepper. Mix together well over the heat. Then stir in the lentils and cool. Mix in the parsley.

Divide the mixture into 12 equal-sized portions and shape into rounds. Coat them in the flour, dip in the lightly beaten egg and then in the combined breadcrumbs and oats (blended until they resemble fine breadcrumbs). Shallow fry in hot oil until golden brown on both sides. Drain well. Serve with yoghourt sauce.

Yoghourt sauce
Combine all the ingredients together and chill until ready to serve.

Serves 6

Chilli burgers

These spicy burgers can be made in advance and fried as required.

Soya beans, soaked overnight 8 oz (225 g)
Large onion, finely chopped 1
Oil 3 tbsp (45 ml)
Garlic cloves, crushed 2
Chilli powder ½ tsp (2.5 ml)
Tomato purée 3 tbsp (45 ml)
Basil, dried ½ tsp (2.5 ml)
Oregano, dried ½ tsp (2.5 ml)
Mixed herbs, dried ¼ tsp (1.25 ml)
Yeast extract 1 tsp (5 ml)
Soya sauce 2 tbsp (30 ml)
Parsley, chopped 3 tbsp (45 ml)
Fresh wholemeal breadcrumbs 2 oz (50 g)
Salt & pepper to taste
100% wholemeal flour, egg & wholemeal breadcrumbs to
   coat
Oil to shallow fry

Preparation time: 20–25 minutes + soaking beans overnight
Cooking time: about 1 hour
Refrigerate: if possible 1–2 hours before frying

Drain the beans and cover them with fresh water. Bring to
the boil. Then simmer gently until tender – about 45 minutes.
Drain and leave to cool. Put the beans into a food processor
and purée them until finely chopped, or alternatively mash
them well. Cook the onion in the oil until transparent and
then stir in the garlic, chilli powder, tomato purée, basil,
oregano and mixed herbs and cook gently for 2 minutes. Put
the onion mixture together with the beans, yeast extract, soya
sauce, parsley, breadcrumbs, salt and pepper into a bowl and
mix thoroughly. Divide the mixture into 10 equal portions
and shape into burgers. Coat lightly in flour, dip in the

lightly beaten egg and coat with the breadcrumbs. Refrigerate if possible for 1–2 hours to allow the burgers to become a little firmer. Cook in a little hot oil until golden on both sides.

Makes 10

Mushroom & herb flan

Wholemeal shortcrust pastry made with 5 oz (150 g) of flour (*see page 22*)
Butter or margarine 1 oz (25 g)
Mushrooms, wiped & sliced 8 oz (225 g)
Spring onions, trimmed & chopped 6
Parsley, chopped 2 tbsp (30 ml)
Ground nutmeg to taste
Salt & pepper to taste
Eggs 3
Soured cream ¼ pt (150 ml)
Milk 4 fl oz (100 ml)

Preparation time: 15 minutes
Cooking time: 40–50 minutes

Roll out the pastry on a lightly floured surface and use to line an 8″ (20 cm) flan tin. Bake 'blind' in the oven at 200°C (400°F/Mark 6) for 10 minutes. Sauté the mushrooms in the butter until just tender. Cool. Sprinkle the finely chopped spring onion and parsley over the flan base. Top with the drained mushrooms and season with nutmeg, salt and pepper. Beat the eggs, soured cream and milk together well and pour into the flan case. Bake in the oven at 190°C (375°F/Mark 5) for 30–40 minutes until the filling has set and is golden brown. Best served warm.

Serves 4–6

Leek & dumpling casserole

Use a large, flameproof casserole or cooking pot with a tight-fitting lid for this warming stew – an excellent main course for cold winter days.

Aduki beans, soaked overnight 4 oz (100 g)
Butter or margarine 2 oz (50 g)
Onion, chopped 1
Garlic cloves, crushed 2
Leeks, trimmed & sliced 1 lb (450 g)
Carrot, diced 1
Mushrooms, wiped & sliced 8 oz (225 g)
Paprika 1 tbsp (15 ml)
Cayenne pepper, pinch
100% wholemeal flour 2 tbsp (30 ml)
Vegetable stock ½ pt (300 ml)
Vegetable stock cube 1
Soya sauce 1 tbsp (15 ml)
Tomato purée 1 tbsp (15 ml)
Tomatoes, chopped 1 lb (450 g)
Salt & pepper to taste
Chopped parsley to garnish

Dumplings
100% wholemeal self raising flour 4 oz (100 g)
Salt ¼ tsp (1.25 ml)
Butter or margarine 1 oz (25 g)
Cheddar cheese, grated 2 oz (50 g)
Parsley, chopped 3 tbsp (45 ml)
Milk 2–3 fl oz (50–75 ml)

Preparation time: 35–40 minutes + soaking beans overnight
Cooking time: about 1½ hours

Drain the beans. Cover with fresh water and cook them until tender, about 30–45 minutes. Drain, reserving the liquid for stock. Heat the butter in a large flameproof casserole, add the onion and cook until transparent. Then add the garlic, leeks, carrot and mushrooms and cook gently for 4–5 minutes until the vegetables have softened slightly. Stir in the paprika, cayenne and flour. Then add the stock, stock cube, soya sauce, tomato purée, chopped tomatoes and salt and pepper to taste. Bring to the boil, cover and simmer gently for 10 minutes. Stir in the beans and bring the mixture back to the boil. Then add the dumplings. Cover with a tight-fitting lid and simmer gently for 20–25 minutes until the dumplings are cooked. The casserole must simmer all the time once the dumplings are added but be careful not to have the heat too high or otherwise it may catch on the bottom. Sprinkle generously with chopped parsley before serving.

Dumplings

Put the flour and salt into a basin. Rub in the butter until it resembles fine crumbs. Then stir in the grated cheese and parsley. Add just enough milk to make a firm dough. Divide into 8 pieces and shape into dumplings.

Serves 4–6

Baked potatoes stuffed with spinach & cheese

Medium-sized potatoes 4
Spinach, washed & coarse stems removed
  12 oz (350 g)
Spring onions, finely chopped 4
Milk 1–2 tbsp (15–30 ml)
Soured cream 4 fl oz (100 ml)
Cheddar cheese, grated 5 oz (150 g)
Parsley, chopped 3 tbsp (45 ml)
Butter or margarine 1 oz (25 g)
Salt & pepper to taste

Ground nutmeg to taste
Paprika & watercress sprigs to garnish

Preparation time: 25 minutes
Cooking time: about 1½ hours

Scrub the potatoes, then put them on to a baking tray and bake in the oven at 200°C (400°F/Mark 6) for approximately 1 hour or until cooked through. Let them cool slightly, then cut in half and scoop out the potato. Reserve the skins. Chop the spinach. Put it in a saucepan with only the water which clings to the leaves and cook until just tender, stirring occasionally. Put the potato into a basin and beat until smooth. Then add the spinach, spring onions, milk, soured cream, half the Cheddar cheese, parsley, butter, salt and pepper and nutmeg, and mix well. Spoon the mixture into the potato shells, top with the remaining grated cheese and bake in the oven at 220°C (425°F/Mark 7) until golden brown – about 20 minutes. Sprinkle with paprika and garnish with watercress.

Serves 4 as a main course
*   8 as a vegetable*

Country cheese & onion flan

One of the first recipes used in Cranks in the early days of Carnaby Street in the 1960s.

Wholemeal shortcrust pastry made with 6 oz (175 g) of flour (*see page 22*)
Cheddar cheese, grated 10 oz (300 g)
Eggs, lightly beaten 2
Milk 12 fl oz (350 ml)
Wholemeal breadcrumbs 1 oz (25 g)
Rolled oats 1 oz (25 g)

Sage, dried ¼ tsp (1.25 ml)
Salt & pepper to taste
Cayenne pepper, large pinch
Garlic clove, crushed 1
French mustard ½ tsp (2.5 ml)
Spring onions, trimmed & sliced 5
Parsley, chopped 2 tbsp (30 ml)

Preparation time: 30 minutes
Cooking time: 40 minutes

Roll out the pastry and use to line a 9″ (23 cm) flan tin. Bake
'blind' in the oven at 200°C (400°F/Mark 6) for 10 minutes
until just lightly browned. Mix together the grated cheese,
lightly beaten eggs, milk, breadcrumbs, oats, sage, salt,
pepper, cayenne, crushed garlic, mustard, spring onions and
parsley. Pour into the pastry case and return to the oven and
continue to bake for approximately 40 minutes, or until the
filling has set and is golden.

Serves 6

Baked stuffed marrow

Marrow 1 about 2½–3 lb (1.125–1.4 kg)
Butter or margarine 1 oz (25 g)
Small onion, finely chopped 1
Garlic clove, crushed 1
100% wholemeal flour 1 tbsp (15 ml)
Firm ripe tomatoes, finely chopped 12 oz (350 g)
Vegetable stock 2 fl oz (50 ml)
Yeast extract 1 tsp (5 ml)
Tomato purée 1 tbsp (15 ml)
Raw brown sugar ½ tsp (2.5 ml)
Fresh mixed herbs, chopped 1 tbsp (15 ml) or dried herbs
  ½ tsp (2.5 ml)
Salt & pepper to taste

Mushrooms, wiped & chopped 4 oz (100 g)
Red or green pepper, deseeded & finely chopped 1
Brown rice, cooked 6 oz (175 g)
Cashew nuts, toasted 1 oz (25 g)
Parsley to garnish

Topping
**Grated cheese 3 oz (75 g) or 100% wholemeal breadcrumbs
2 oz (50 g), chopped mixed nuts, toasted 1 oz (25 g), &
butter or margarine ½ oz (15 g)**

Preparation time: 25–30 minutes
Cooking time: 40–50 minutes

Cut the marrow in half lengthways and scoop out the seeds.
(These may be used in a soup or casserole, provided they are
from young marrows). Place both halves into a large pan of
boiling water. Bring back to the boil quickly. Then simmer
for 1–2 minutes. Drain and rinse under cold water to stop
further cooking. Dry the marrow thoroughly with kitchen
paper.

Melt the butter in a saucepan, add the finely chopped
onion and cook until transparent. Stir in the garlic and flour.
Add the finely chopped tomatoes, stock, yeast extract, tomato
purée, sugar, herbs, salt and pepper. Cook gently, covered,
for about 3 minutes. Then add the mushrooms and the
pepper and simmer uncovered for a further 3 minutes, stirring
occasionally. Add the rice and the nuts and season to taste.

Spoon the rice mixture into the marrow shells and place
them side by side in a baking dish. Sprinkle with grated
cheese or with the mixed breadcrumbs, chopped nuts and
melted butter. Bake in the oven at 190°C (375°F/Mark 5) for
about 30–40 minutes, until the filling is heated through and
the marrow is tender. Serve garnished with parsley.

Serves 4–6

Brazil & cashew nut roast with chestnut stuffing & red wine sauce

Serve this at Christmas or for any celebration – the ribbon of chestnut stuffing makes it extra special.

Butter or margarine 3 oz (75 g)
Medium-sized onion, finely chopped 1
Garlic clove, crushed 1
Celery sticks, finely chopped 5
Brazil nuts, finely ground 6 oz (175 g)
Cashew nuts, toasted & finely ground (*see page 20*)
  6 oz (175 g)
Flaked millet 2 oz (50 g)
Wholemeal breadcrumbs 2 oz (50 g)
Potato or parsnip, cooked & mashed 4 oz (100 g)
Parsley, chopped 2 tbsp (30 ml)
Sage, dried 1 tsp (5 ml)
Oregano, dried ½ tsp (2.5 ml)
Ground ginger ¼ tsp (1.25 ml)
Cayenne pepper ¼ tsp (1.25 ml)
Curry powder (optional) ½ tsp (2.5 ml)
Lemon, rind & juice of ½
Egg, lightly beaten 1
Stock or white wine to mix
Salt & pepper to taste
Chestnut purée 8 oz (225 g)

Preparation time: about 1 hour
Cooking time: about 1 hour

Heat the butter in a small saucepan, add the onion and cook until transparent. Then add the garlic and finely chopped celery and continue to cook for 1 minute. Remove from the heat and put in a large bowl together with the finely ground brazil nuts, cashew nuts, millet, breadcrumbs, mashed potato, parsley, herbs and spices, lemon rind and juice, lightly beaten egg and stock. Season generously with salt and pepper and mix well to give a firm consistency. Press half the mixture into a greaseproof paper-lined 2 lb loaf tin. Spread the chestnut purée evenly over the mixture. Then top with the remaining half of nut mixture. Bake in the oven at 190°C (375°F/Mark 5) for 45 minutes–1 hour, or until golden brown. Serve sliced, with Red wine sauce or Brown onion gravy.

Nutties (*to serve with drinks*)
Make half the quantity of the nut mixture and shape into 24 small balls. Fry in shallow fat until golden all over. Drain on kitchen paper. Serve warm or cold.

Serves 6–8

Red wine sauce

Butter or margarine 1 oz (25 g)
Medium-sized onion, finely chopped 1
100% wholemeal flour 2 tbsp (30 ml)
Ripe tomatoes, chopped 3
Dry red wine ½ pt (300 ml)
Vegetable stock ¼ pt (150 ml)
Vegetable stock concentrate or yeast extract to taste
Salt & pepper to taste
Parsley, chopped 2 tbsp (30 ml)

Preparation time: 10 minutes
Cooking time: 25 minutes

Melt the butter and sauté the onion until well browned. Stir in the flour and cook for 1 minute. Add the tomatoes, wine and stock and simmer, covered, for 20 minutes. Then add the vegetable stock concentrate and salt and pepper to taste. Stir in the chopped parsley before serving. For a thicker consistency simmer for a little while uncovered to reduce the sauce.

Makes about 1 pt (600 ml)

Brown onion gravy

Oil 3 tbsp (45 ml)
Medium-sized onions, thinly sliced 2
100% wholemeal flour 2 tbsp (30 ml)
Vegetable stock ¾ pt (450 ml)
Red wine (optional) 2 tbsp (30 ml)
Tomato purée 2 tsp (10 ml)
Yeast extract 1 tsp (5 ml)
Vegetable stock cube 1
Salt & pepper to taste

Preparation time: 8–10 minutes
Cooking time: 10–15 minutes

Heat the oil in a frying pan, add the onion and cook until golden brown. Stir in the flour and cook for 1–2 minutes, stirring all the time. Add the stock, wine, tomato purée, yeast extract, stock cube, salt and pepper. Bring to the boil, then simmer very gently for 5 minutes.

Baked avocado filled with chilli, tomato & cheese

It's unusual to find hot avocado recipes. For grilling, topped with cheese and breadcrumbs, or for baking, it is essential to use ripe avocados. In this dish the spicy Mexican chilli contrasts with the smooth creaminess of the avocado. The sauce may be made in advance but don't cut the avocados until required. Corn chips go well with this.

Oil 1 tbsp (15 ml)
Small onion, finely chopped 1
Garlic clove, crushed 1
Chilli powder, large pinch
Ground cumin ¼ tsp (1.25 ml)
Firm, ripe tomatoes, finely chopped 8 oz (225 g)
Tomato purée 1 tbsp (15 ml)
Green pepper, deseeded & diced ½
Spring onions, trimmed & sliced 2
Mushrooms, wiped & chopped 2 oz (50 g)
Salt & pepper to taste
Large ripe avocados 2
Cheddar cheese, grated 2 oz (50 g)
Watercress or fresh coriander to garnish

Preparation time: about 20 minutes
Cooking time: about 15 minutes

Heat the oil in a small saucepan and fry the onion until transparent. Then add the garlic, chilli powder, cumin, chopped tomatoes, tomato purée, pepper, spring onions and mushrooms. Season to taste and simmer gently until the mixture is very thick, stirring from time to time to prevent it from sticking. Cut the avocados in half and remove the stones. Place on a heatproof dish and spoon the tomato mixture into the 4 avocado halves. (Alternatively, scoop the flesh out of the avocado skins and dice it. Mix carefully with the sauce, then pile back into the skins). Top with the grated cheese. Bake in the oven at 220°C (425°F/Mark 7) for 10–15 minutes until the cheese has melted and the avocado is hot. Serve garnished with watercress.

Serves 4

Rice & vegetable bake

This tasty rice and vegetable dish with a cheese topping can be made in advance and reheated as required. Serve with salad or a green vegetable.

Base
Butter or margarine 1 oz (25 g)
Small onion, finely chopped 1
Long grain brown rice 6 oz (175 g)
Vegetable stock, or water & vegetable stock cube
  ¾ pt (450 ml)
Egg, lightly beaten 1
Salt & pepper to taste

Filling
Butter or margarine 1 oz (25 g)
Leek, trimmed & sliced 1
Garlic cloves, crushed 2
Mushrooms, wiped & sliced 4 oz (100 g)
Red pepper, deseeded & diced 1
Medium-sized courgette, sliced 1
Tomatoes, chopped 8 oz (225 g)
Salt & pepper to taste

Topping
Butter or margarine 1 oz (25 g)
100% wholemeal flour 1 oz (25 g)
Milk 9 fl oz (275 ml)
Cheddar cheese, grated 5 oz (150 g)
Egg, lightly beaten 1
Ground nutmeg ¼ tsp (1.25 ml)
Salt & pepper to taste

Preparation time: 45 minutes
Cooking time: 1¼ hours

Base
Melt the butter in a pan, add the finely chopped onion and

cook until transparent. Add the rice and vegetable stock. Bring to the boil, then simmer gently, covered, for 30–40 minutes or until the rice is cooked and the liquid all absorbed – if necessary add a little more water to prevent the rice sticking. Cool. Then stir in the lightly beaten egg. Season with salt and pepper to taste. Press the rice mixture over the base of a well greased 9″ (23 cm) square ovenproof dish.

Filling

Melt the butter in a frying pan, add the sliced leek and garlic and cook for 1 minute. Then add the mushrooms and diced pepper and cook for a further minute. Finally, add the sliced courgette and tomato and continue to cook until the vegetables are just tender – about 5 minutes. Season with salt and pepper. Arrange over the rice base.

Topping

Melt the butter in a pan. Stir in the flour and cook over a gentle heat for 1 minute. Add the milk and stir until the sauce boils and thickens. Remove from the heat. Stir in half the grated cheese. Allow to cool slightly. Then add the lightly beaten egg, nutmeg and salt and pepper to taste. Pour over the vegetable filling and top with the remaining grated cheese.

Bake in the oven at 190°C (375°F/Mark 5) for 25–30 minutes until golden.

Serves 6

Potato & courgette fritters

These are irresistible – try one and you'll want more! We serve them with fresh tomato sauce.

Medium-sized potatoes 2 or 12 oz (350 g)
Medium-sized courgettes 2 or 12 oz (350 g)
Eggs, lightly beaten 2

Appetizers & starters

1 Melon & grapefruit with ginger & sherry dressing
2 Fresh asparagus & egg mousse
3 Herbed cheesejacks
4 Leek & avocado vinaigrette
5 Nut & wine pâté
6 Herb cheese pâté
7 Bread tartlets with mushroom filling

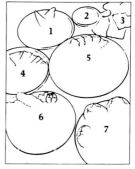

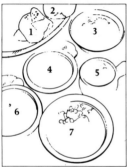

Soups

1. Sesame seed knots
2. Potato soda bread
3. Sweetcorn chowder
4. Tomato & orange soup
5. Iced borscht
6. Cream of spinach & coconut soup
7. Bean & tomato soup

Salads & dressings

1 Bean sprout salad
2 Flageolet bean & avocado salad
3 Wholewheat salad
4 Spinach & pine kernel salad
5 Oriental salad
6 Melon and butter bean salad

Main dishes

1 Gougère
2 Leek & dumpling
   casserole
3 Corn bread
4 Tofu & cashew nuts in
   sweet & sour sauce
5 Harvest pancake pie
6 Baked avocado filled with
   chilli, tomato & cheese
7 Brazil & cashew nut roast
   with chestnut stuffing
   & red wine sauce
8 Green lentil rissoles with
   yoghourt sauce

Vegetables

1 Green beans Italian style
2 Viennese red cabbage
3 Sautéed root vegetables
   with lime
4 Mange-tout with peppers,
   ginger & garlic
5 Courgette & tomato
   ramekins
6 Glazed carrots

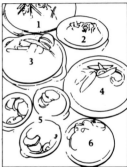

Puddings & desserts

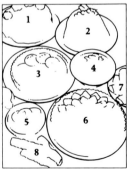

1 Carob meringue gâteau
2 Summer pudding
3 Fresh lemon tart
4 Fresh fruit salad
5 Poached plums with
   cinnamon cream
6 Strawberry coconut flan
7 Sponge fingers
8 Honey snaps

Cakes & biscuits

1 Savoury scone crescent
2 Continental fruit plait
3 Lemon madeira cake
4 Cranks party cake
5 Fruit & nut cake
6 Carob almond cake
7 Coconut fruit mince slice
8 Fudge brownies
9 Honey & sesame seed squares
10 Muesli biscuits
11 Hazelnut carob biscuits

Drinks

1 White wine cup
2 Cider punch
3 Luaka tea punch
4 Mixed fruit cup
5 Pineapple coconut crush
6 Strawberry orange blush
7 Mulled wine

Salt & pepper to taste
Ground nutmeg to taste
Oil 2 tbsp (30 ml)
Butter or margarine 1 oz (25 g)

Preparation time: 15 minutes
Cooking time: about 15–20 minutes

Grate the potatoes and courgettes on the coarse side of the grater. Then, using your hands, squeeze out as much of the liquid from them as possible. Or place the grated vegetables on a clean tea towel and wring the excess juices out. Put the pulp into a basin with the lightly beaten eggs. Season with salt, pepper and nutmeg, and mix together well. Heat the oil in a medium-sized frying pan, then add the butter. When hot, spoon large tablespoonfuls of the mixture into the pan. Flatten each fritter slightly using a fork. Cook over a medium heat until brown, then carefully turn to cook the other side. Repeat using the remaining mixture. It may be necessary to add a little more oil to the pan to cook the second batch.

Serves 4

Wholemeal pancakes

These may be made in advance and freeze very well. If you are going to freeze them add a couple of tablespoons of oil to the mixture before making the pancakes. Interleave them with greaseproof paper before freezing.

100% wholemeal flour 8 oz (225 g)
Salt, pinch
Eggs 2
Milk ¾ pt (450 ml)

Preparation time: 10 minutes + 30 minutes for batter to stand
Cooking time: about 25 minutes

Put the flour and salt into a basin, add the eggs and a little of the milk. Whisk until the mixture is smooth and free of lumps. Gradually add the rest of the milk to make a smooth batter – if necessary add a little more milk if it seems too thick. Allow to stand for 30 minutes. Pour the batter into a jug. Heat an 8 ″ (20 cm) pancake pan and grease it well. Pour about 3 tablespoons of batter into the pan, swirling it around evenly. Cook the pancake over a medium heat until light golden brown. Turn and cook the other side. Repeat until the batter is all used up.

Alternative
Buckwheat pancakes
Use half wholemeal flour and half buckwheat flour.

Makes 8–10 pancakes

Pancakes stuffed with ratatouille

Savoury pancakes can be made with a variety of different fillings. They are ideal for a large number of guests as they can be made and filled in advance and reheated just before serving. Red or White wine sauce goes well with them.

Aubergine 1
Oil 2 tbsp (30 ml)
Onion, sliced 1
Red pepper, deseeded & diced 1
Green pepper, deseeded & diced 1
Courgettes, sliced 3
Water 2 fl oz (50 ml)
Vegetable stock cube 1
Tomato purée 2 tbsp (30 ml)
Garlic cloves, crushed 2
Mixed herbs, dried ½ tsp (2.5 ml)
Salt & pepper to taste

Tomatoes, sliced 5
100% wholemeal pancakes (*see page 129*) 8–10
Cheddar cheese, grated 2 oz (50 g)
Watercress to garnish

Preparation time: 40 minutes
Cooking time: about 45 minutes

Cut the aubergine into cubes and put it in salted water for 30 minutes. Drain, rinse, and dry on kitchen paper. Heat the oil in a large saucepan, add the sliced onion and cook gently until transparent. Place the remaining vegetables on top of the onion in layers. First the aubergine, then the peppers, then the courgettes. Mix together the water, stock cube, tomato purée, garlic, herbs, salt and pepper and pour over the vegetables. Then cover with the sliced tomatoes. Cover the pan tightly and simmer gently for about 15–20 minutes, or until the vegetables are tender. Drain off the liquid and reserve it for soups and sauces. Divide the mixture between the pancakes. Roll up. Place in an ovenproof dish, sprinkle with grated cheese and bake in the oven at 180°C (350°F/ Mark 4) for about 20–30 minutes or until heated through. Serve garnished with watercress.

Serves 8–10

Spinach, cheese & tomato pancakes

Spinach, washed & coarse stems removed 2 lb (900 g)
100% wholemeal pancakes (*see page 129*) 8–10
Chopped parsley to garnish

Sauce
Medium-sized onion, finely chopped 1
Butter or margarine 1 oz (25 g)
100% wholemeal flour 2 tbsp (30 ml)
Ripe tomatoes, finely chopped 1½ lb (675 g)

Tomato purée 3 tbsp (45 ml)
Garlic cloves, crushed 2
Ground nutmeg to taste
Vegetable stock cube 1
Salt & pepper to taste
Cheddar cheese, grated 4 oz (100 g)

Preparation time: 40 minutes
Cooking time: about 40 minutes

Chop the spinach roughly and put it into a saucepan with only the water that clings to the leaves. Cook over a medium heat until just tender, stirring occasionally to prevent it from sticking. Mix the spinach with approximately three-quarters of the sauce and divide this mixture between the pancakes. Roll up and place in an ovenproof dish. Spoon the remaining sauce over the top. Bake in the oven at 180°C (350°F/Mark 4) for about 20–30 minutes or until heated through. Garnish with chopped parsley.

Sauce
Cook the onion in the butter until transparent. Stir in the flour, then cook for a minute. Add the tomatoes to the onion mixture and stir over the heat until the sauce boils and thickens. Then add the tomato purée, garlic, nutmeg, stock cube and salt and pepper. Simmer gently for 2 minutes. Stir in the cheese and allow to melt. Remove from the heat immediately.

Serves 8–10

Harvest pancake pie

Although this recipe may be time-consuming, it is well worth the effort – an impressive dish for any dinner table.

100% wholemeal pancakes (*see page 129*) 8–10
Cheddar cheese, grated 3 oz (75 g)

Courgette filling
Butter or margarine 1 oz (25 g)
Courgettes, thinly sliced 1 lb (450 g)
Onion, finely chopped 1
Garlic clove, crushed 1
Tomatoes, finely chopped 1 lb (450 g)
Tomato purée 1 tbsp (15 ml)
Yeast extract 1 tsp (5 ml)
Fresh mixed herbs, chopped 1 tbsp (15 ml)
  or dried mixed herbs 1 tsp (5 ml)
Parsley, chopped 1 tbsp (15 ml)
Salt & pepper to taste

Mushroom filling
Butter or margarine 1½ oz (40 g)
Mushrooms, wiped & sliced 1 lb (450 g)
Garlic clove, crushed 1
100% wholemeal flour 4 tbsp (60 ml)
Milk 7 fl oz (200 ml)
Salt & pepper to taste
Parsley, chopped 2 tbsp (30 ml)
Spring onions, trimmed & sliced 6
Double cream 2 tbsp (30 ml)

Preparation time: about 1 hour
Cooking time: 45–50 minutes

Courgette filling
Melt the butter in a medium-sized frying pan. Add the courgettes and sauté until just tender. Remove them from the pan, leaving behind all the buttery juices. Add the finely chopped onion and cook until transparent. Then add the garlic, chopped tomato, tomato purée and yeast extract (stir in the dried herbs now if they are used). Simmer this sauce until thick – about 5–10 minutes, stirring occasionally to

prevent it from sticking. Remove from the heat and stir in the courgettes and fresh herbs. Adjust seasoning to taste.

Mushroom filling

Melt the butter in a medium-sized frying pan and add the finely sliced mushrooms. Cook for a few minutes until just tender. Stir in the garlic and flour, cook for a minute, then add the milk. Stir until the sauce boils and thickens. Season with salt and pepper and simmer very gently for 1–2 minutes. Remove from the heat and mix in the finely chopped spring onions, parsley and cream.

Place one pancake on a shallow, heatproof serving dish. Spread with some of the courgette mixture, sprinkle with a little grated cheese, then cover with another pancake. Spread some of the mushroom mixture evenly over this pancake, then top with another pancake. Continue the layers, finishing with a pancake and using up all the filling. Sprinkle the top of the pie with a little grated cheese. Bake in the oven at 190°C (375°F/Mark 5) for 20–30 minutes until thoroughly heated through. Cut into wedges and serve with White wine sauce (*see page below*).

Serves 6–8

White wine sauce

A delicious sauce that goes particularly well with pancakes. Any prepared vegetables can be stirred into a thickened sauce and used as a filling.

Butter or margarine 1 oz (25 g)
100% wholemeal flour 2 tbsp (30 ml)
Milk ½ pt (300 ml)
Dry white wine ¼ pt (150 ml)
Bayleaf 1

Ground nutmeg, large pinch
Salt & pepper to taste

Preparation time: 5 minutes
Cooking time: 10 minutes

Melt the butter, add the flour and mix well. Cook for 1 minute stirring all the time. Stir in the milk and then the wine. Add the bayleaf and nutmeg and simmer gently for 5 minutes, stirring occasionally. Adjust seasoning to taste and remove the bayleaf before serving.

Alternatives

French onion sauce Sauté 4 oz (100 g) chopped onion in 1 oz (25 g) butter until golden and add to the White wine sauce. Purée in a liquidizer goblet if wished.

Mushroom sauce Sauté 4 oz (100 g) chopped mushrooms in 1 oz (25 g) butter and add to the White wine sauce.

Lemon & herb sauce Add 3 tbsp (45 ml) chopped fresh herbs – parsley, mint, chives, tarragon – and 1 tsp (5 ml) freshly grated lemon rind, and lemon juice to taste, to the made White wine sauce.

Makes about ⅔ pt (400 ml)

Vegetables

Glazed carrots

This is an interesting way to serve carrots and the dash of cream gives an added richness. Alternatively, leave out the cream and use 1 tablespoon of coarse-grain or French mustard instead.

Butter or margarine 1 oz (25 g)
Small onion, finely chopped 1
Carrots, thinly sliced 1 lb (450 g)
Vegetable stock ¼ pt (150 ml)
Honey 1 tsp (5 ml)
Double cream (optional) 2 tbsp (30 ml)
Salt & pepper to taste
Chopped parsley to garnish

Preparation time: 10–15 minutes
Cooking time: about 15 minutes

Heat the butter in a large saucepan and cook the finely chopped onion until transparent. Do not allow it to brown. Add the carrots, stock and honey. Cover the pan and cook gently until the carrots are almost tender – about 10 minutes. Remove the lid, and continue to cook for a further 5 minutes until the liquid is all used up. Season with salt and pepper and add the cream. Toss the carrots over the heat until the cream has reduced slightly and coats the carrots. Serve sprinkled with parsley.

Serves 4

Pumpkin

These two dishes are perfect for Hallowe'en. Pumpkin has a delicate flavour which can be enhanced with chopped herbs, or spices such as ground nutmeg or mace.

Whole pumpkin, about 2 lb (900 g)
Butter or margarine 1 oz (25 g)
Salt & pepper to taste
Nutmeg to taste

Preparation time: 15 minutes
Cooking time: 30–45 minutes

Baked whole pumpkin

Cut the top off the pumpkin and scoop out the seeds. Season the cavity with salt and freshly milled black pepper, and add the butter. Cover with the pumpkin lid. Put the pumpkin into a small baking dish and pour in ½ pint (300 ml) water. Bake in the oven at 200°C (400°F/Mark 6) for about 30 minutes or until tender.

Creamed pumpkin

Cut the pumpkin into wedges and scoop out the seeds. Arrange on a baking tray and bake for 30–45 minutes, until tender when tested with a skewer. (Alternatively, peel and dice and steam for about 20 minutes.) Scoop the pumpkin flesh from the skin and mash or purée in a blender goblet or food processor. Stir in the butter and season to taste with salt, pepper and grated nutmeg.

Serves 4

Green beans Italian style

Beans go particularly well with a garlic and tomato sauce. Be careful not to overcook, the beans should be crisp.

Green beans, topped & tailed 12 oz (350 g)
Oil 1 tbsp (15 ml)
Garlic cloves, crushed 2
Tomatoes, finely chopped 8 oz (225 g)
Tomato purée 1 tbsp (15 ml)
Salt & pepper to taste
Fresh basil or parsley, chopped 1 tbsp (15 ml)

Preparation time: 15 minutes
Cooking time: about 10–15 minutes

Steam the beans or cook in boiling water, until just tender, about 5–10 minutes, depending on their size.

Heat the oil in a medium-sized saucepan and add the garlic, tomatoes, tomato purée and the salt and pepper to taste. Simmer gently until the sauce becomes thick, about 5 minutes. Then stir in the basil or parsley. Toss the beans in the sauce until hot. Serve immediately.

Serves 4

Leeks with cheese & watercress sauce

The pale green colour of this sauce blends well with the leeks. If maize flour is used, as an alternative to wholemeal flour, it makes a slightly paler sauce.

Leeks 1 lb (450 g)
Vegetable stock 1 pt (600 ml)
Butter or margarine 1 oz (25 g)
100% wholemeal flour or maize flour 2 tbsp (30 ml)
Milk ¼ pt (150 ml)
Salt & pepper to taste
Cheddar cheese, grated 3 oz (75 g)
Watercress 1 bunch

Preparation time: 20 minutes
Cooking time: about 10 minutes

Trim the leeks leaving most of the green part. Cut them in half lengthways and wash them thoroughly. Put the stock into a large pan and bring to the boil. Add the leeks, cutting them in half if they are large, and simmer gently until tender – about 5–8 minutes. Drain well, reserving ¼ pint (150 ml) of the stock. Put the leeks into a serving dish, cover and keep warm.

Melt the butter in a small pan, stir in the flour and cook for a minute, stirring all the time. Stir in the milk and the reserved stock. Stir over the heat until the sauce boils and thickens. Then simmer gently for a minute or two. Remove from the heat, stir in the cheese and season to taste.

Remove the leaves from the watercress, reserving some sprigs for a garnish, and put them into the liquidizer goblet or food processor. Add the sauce and blend to make a pale green sauce. Return to the saucepan and reheat gently. Pour the sauce over the leeks and garnish with watercress.

Serves 3–4

Broccoli with butter & flaked almonds

Broccoli 1½ lb (675 g)
Butter or margarine 1 oz (25 g)
Toasted flaked almonds (*see page 20*) 1 oz (25 g)

Preparation time: 10 minutes
Cooking time: 10 minutes

Trim the broccoli, removing any coarse skin from the stems with a potato peeler. Steam or cook in boiling water until just tender, about 5–10 minutes. Drain well. Then toss in the melted butter and sprinkle with the flaked almonds.

Serves 4

Cabbage with apple & juniper berries

This goes well with Rice & vegetable bake or Curried lentil pie.

White cabbage 2 lb (900 g)
Butter or margarine 2 oz (50 g)
Onion, finely chopped 1
Garlic clove, crushed 1
Juniper berries, crushed 12
Cooking apples, cored & diced 2
Sultanas 2 oz (50 g)
Salt & pepper to taste
Chopped parsley to garnish

Preparation time: 25 minutes
Cooking time: about 25 minutes

Wash the cabbage and shred it finely. Heat the butter in a large, heavy-based saucepan. Add the onion and cook until transparent. Then add the crushed garlic and juniper berries. Cook for a few seconds. Then stir in the cabbage, chopped apple and the sultanas. Season with salt and pepper. Cover the pan and cook gently until tender – about 20 minutes, stirring occasionally to prevent the cabbage from sticking. If necessary add a little vegetable stock or water. Serve sprinkled with parsley.

Serves 6–8

Broad beans in creamy herb sauce

Broad beans, in their pods 3 lb (1.35 kg)
Butter or margarine 1oz (25 g)
100% wholemeal flour 2 tbsp (30 ml)
Milk ¼ pt (150 ml)
Salt & freshly milled pepper to taste
Ground nutmeg to taste
Fresh herbs, chopped (basil, marjoram, chives, parsley, thyme) 4 tbsp (60 ml)

Preparation time: 20 minutes
Cooking time: 8–10 minutes

Shell the beans and steam or cook them in boiling water for 5–10 minutes, until tender. Drain, reserving ¼ pint (150 ml) of the liquid.

Heat the butter in a medium-sized pan and stir in the flour. Cook gently for 1 minute, stirring. Then remove from the heat and stir in the milk and reserved liquid. Stir over the heat until the sauce boils and thickens. Season to taste with salt, pepper and nutmeg. Add the beans, and a little more cooking liquid if the sauce is too thick. Allow the beans to heat through and then stir in the herbs.

Serves 4

Courgette & tomato ramekins

This is a very attractive vegetable dish for a dinner party.

Oil 2 tbsp (30 ml)
Medium-sized onion, sliced 1
Mushrooms, sliced 4 oz (100 g)
Garlic clove, crushed 1
Small courgettes, sliced 8 oz (225 g)
Tomatoes, sliced 2

Butter or margarine ½ oz (15 g)
Salt & pepper to taste

Preparation time: 25 minutes
Cooking time: about 30 minutes

Heat the oil and sauté the onion, mushrooms and garlic until golden. Season well and divide into 4 ovenproof ramekins, or a round, ovenproof dish. Arrange the slices of courgette and tomato in a circular pattern on the top. Dot with butter, season with salt and pepper and bake at 200°C (400°F/Mark 6) for about 15–20 minutes until the courgettes are tender.

Serves 4

Spiced cauliflower with tomato

This can be prepared in advance, refrigerated and served cold for a buffet. It also makes an excellent starter served with pitta bread.

Medium-sized cauliflower 1
Oil 2 tbsp (30 ml)
Small onion, finely chopped 1
Ground cumin 1 tsp (5 ml)
Whole cumin seed 1 tsp (5 ml)
Cardamom pods, crushed (just use seeds) 4
Ground coriander 1 tsp (5 ml)
Chilli powder ¼ tsp (1.25 ml)
Curry powder ¼ tsp (1.25 ml)
Turmeric ¼ tsp (1.25 ml)
Garlic cloves, crushed 2
Tomatoes, finely chopped 12 oz (350 g)
Lemon juice 1 tbsp (15 ml)
Salt & pepper to taste
Chopped parsley to garnish

Preparation time: 15 minutes
Cooking time: 10–15 minutes

Cut the cauliflower into small florets. Plunge into boiling water, bring back to the boil, then rinse in cold running water.

Heat the oil in a pan and cook the onion until transparent. Add the spices and garlic and stir over the heat for a minute. Then add the tomato and cook for 1 minute before adding the lemon juice and cauliflower. Season with salt and pepper. Cook gently, stirring occasionally, until the cauliflower is just tender, about 5 minutes. Take care not to overcook it. Serve sprinkled with chopped parsley.

Serves 4–6

Mange-tout with peppers, ginger & garlic

This colourful dish goes well as an accompaniment to Gougère – a stunning combination for a special meal.

Oil 2 tbsp (30 ml)
Garlic cloves, crushed 2
Fresh green ginger, grated, or ground ginger 1 tsp (5 ml)
Mange-tout peas, topped & tailed 8 oz (225 g)
Large red pepper, deseeded & thinly sliced 1
Large yellow or green pepper, deseeded & thinly sliced 1
Salt & pepper to taste

Preparation time: 15 minutes
Cooking time: 5 minutes

Heat the oil in a frying pan or wok. Add the crushed garlic and ginger. Then stir in the mange-tout and peppers. Toss over a medium heat for 2–3 minutes until the vegetables are just tender but still crisp. Season with salt and pepper and serve immediately.

Serves 3–4

Fresh peas with onion & lettuce

Fresh peas, in their pods, 2 lb (900 g)
Butter or margarine 2 oz (50 g)
Spring onions, trimmed & sliced 4
Cos lettuce, shredded ½
Salt & pepper to taste

Preparation time: 20 minutes
Cooking time: 15 minutes

Shell the peas and steam or cook them in boiling water until just tender – about 10 minutes. Heat the butter in a pan and add the sliced spring onions. Cook until tender. Add the drained peas and shredded lettuce. Season with salt and pepper and toss over a medium heat until heated through. Serve immediately.

Serves 4

Spiced okra

This highly spiced dish makes an excellent starter, or is good served with lentil rissoles or jacket potatoes.

Okra 12 oz (350 g)
Oil 2 tbsp (30 ml)
Fresh green ginger, grated 1 tsp (5 ml)
Small fresh chilli, finely chopped 1
Garlic cloves, crushed 2

Cumin seeds 1 tsp (5 ml)
Ground coriander 1 tsp (5 ml)
Tomatoes, chopped 1 lb (450 g)
Salt & pepper to taste
Fresh coriander or parsley, chopped 2 tbsp (30 ml)

Preparation time: 15 minutes
Cooking time: about 15 minutes

Wash and top and tail the okra. Heat the oil in a frying pan and add the ginger, chilli, garlic and the spices. Stir over a medium heat for a few seconds. Then add the tomatoes and season to taste. Cover the pan and simmer very gently for 2 minutes until the tomatoes have softened a little. Add the okra and cook gently until they are tender, about 5–10 minutes. Stir in the coriander or parsley and serve.

Serves 4

Herbed potato bake

Potatoes 1½ lb (675 g)
Butter or margarine 1 oz (25 g)
Milk ¼ pt (150 ml)
Soured cream 2 tbsp (30 ml)
Spring onions, chopped 4
Chives, chopped 2 tbsp (30 ml)
Salt & pepper to taste
Cheddar cheese, grated 1 oz (25 g)
Paprika to garnish

Preparation time: 20 minutes
Cooking time: 40–50 minutes

Cut the potatoes into quarters if large and cook in boiling salted water until tender – about 15–20 minutes. Drain and mash, beating in the butter and hot milk. Add a little more milk if the mixture seems too dry. Then add the soured cream, chopped spring onions and chives, salt and pepper and mix well. Pile the mixture into an ovenproof serving dish and top with the grated cheese. Bake in the oven at 190°C (375°F/Mark 5) for 20–30 minutes until heated through and lightly browned on top. Sprinkle with paprika.

Serves 4

Sautéed root vegetables with lime

Mixed root vegetables 1½ lb (675 g)
Butter or margarine 1 oz (25 g)
Fresh ginger, grated 1 tsp (5 ml)
Lime, juice of 1
Salt & pepper to taste
Chopped parsley & lime slices to garnish

Preparation time: about 25 minutes
Cooking time: about 10 minutes

Prepare the vegetables (potatoes, carrots, parsnips, salsify, swedes, turnips) and cut into chunky sticks about ½" (1 cm) wide and 3" (7.5 cm) long. Steam or boil for 5–7 minutes until almost tender. Melt the butter in a saucepan, add the drained vegetables and the lime juice and season. Cook gently, stirring, for 2-3 minutes until the vegetables are well glazed. Serve sprinkled with chopped parsley and garnish with fresh lime.

Serves 4

Potatoes boulangère

This is always popular in our 'Dine and Wine' evening restaurant.

Butter or margarine 1 oz (25 g)
Large onion, thinly sliced 1

Potatoes, thinly sliced 2 lb (900 g)
Salt & pepper to taste
Ground nutmeg to taste
Cheddar cheese, grated (optional) 4 oz (100 g)
Vegetable stock ½ pt (300 ml)

Preparation time: 25 minutes
Cooking time: 1½ hours

Melt the butter in a frying pan and cook the onion gently for 5 minutes until softened. Arrange a layer of the sliced potatoes over the base of an ovenproof dish. Cover with a little of the onion. Sprinkle with grated cheese and season with salt, pepper and nutmeg. Continue the layers, finishing with potato and grated cheese. Pour the stock evenly over the top. Cover with foil and bake in the oven at 180°C (350°F/Mark 4) for approximately 1 hour or until the potatoes are tender. Remove the foil and continue to cook until the top is golden – about 20 minutes.

Serves 6

Viennese red cabbage

This colourful vegetable dish can be served hot or cold.

Oil 1 tbsp (15 ml)
Onion, chopped 1
Red cabbage, chopped 1 lb (450 g)
Cooking apple, cored & diced 1
Cider vinegar 2 tbsp (30 ml)
Raw brown sugar 1 tbsp (15 ml)
Red wine 6 fl oz (175 ml)
Salt & pepper to taste

Preparation time: 20 minutes
Cooking time: 35–50 minutes

Heat the oil in a large saucepan and sauté the onion until transparent. Add the remaining ingredients. Cover and simmer gently for about 30–45 minutes, according to taste. Stir occasionally, and add a little water if necessary to prevent the cabbage sticking.

Serves 4–6

Creamed spinach

Fresh spinach 2 lb (900 g)
Butter or margarine ½ oz (15 g)
100% wholemeal flour 1 tbsp (15 ml)
Salt & pepper to taste
Ground nutmeg to taste
Double cream 2 tbsp (30 ml)

Preparation time: 25 minutes
Cooking time: 10 minutes

Wash the spinach thoroughly and remove any coarse stems. Put it into a saucepan with only the water which clings to the leaves. Cover and cook until tender, giving it a stir once or twice. Drain well, reserving any liquid and make up to ¼ pt (150 ml) with vegetable stock or water.

Heat the butter in a small saucepan and stir in the flour. Cook for a few seconds, then add the reserved liquid. Stir over the heat until the sauce boils and thickens. Season to taste with salt, pepper and nutmeg. Remove from the heat and add the cream. Put the spinach and the sauce in a blender or food processor, and blend until fine but not mushy. Return to the saucepan and allow to heat through.

Serves 3–4

Steamed carrots with caraway

Carrots, coarsely grated 1 lb (450 g)
Butter or margarine 1 oz (25 g)
Caraway seeds 1 tsp (5 ml)
Lemon juice 2 tsp (10 ml)
Salt & pepper to taste

Preparation time: 15 minutes
Cooking time: about 10 minutes

Steam the carrots for 8–10 minutes until just tender. Melt
the butter and fry the caraway seeds for a few seconds, until
the butter turns golden. Combine all the ingredients together
and season to taste.

Serves 4

Onions in red wine

Butter or margarine 1 oz (25 g)
Large onions, quartered 3 about 1½ lb (675 g)
Raw pale brown sugar 2 tbsp (30 ml)
Thyme, dried 1 tsp (5 ml)
Red wine ⅓ pt (200 ml)
Salt & pepper to taste
Chopped parsley to garnish

Preparation time: 10 minutes
Cooking time: about 45 minutes

Melt the butter in a heavy-based saucepan and brown the
onions well on all sides. Add the sugar and stir well to coat
the onions evenly. Pour in the red wine, bring to the boil,
reduce the heat, cover and simmer for 15 minutes. Remove
the lid and continue to simmer gently for a further 25–30

minutes, stirring occasionally until the liquid is reduced to a glaze. Season to taste and serve sprinkled with chopped parsley.

Serves 4

Bunches of beans with herb butter

A very simple but attractive way of serving French beans.

Thin green beans, topped & tailed 1 lb (450 g)
Small red pepper 1

Herb butter
Butter or margarine 2 oz (50 g)
Garlic clove, crushed 1
Fresh chopped herbs (thyme, mint, chives, tarragon)
 2 tbsp (30 ml)
Lemon juice 1 tsp (6 ml)
Freshly milled black pepper

Preparation time: 25 minutes
Cooking time: 10–15 minutes

Steam the beans until just tender – about 10 minutes. Cut 6 rings from the centre of the pepper and fill each one with a bunch of beans. Serve with Herb butter.

Herb butter
This freezes very well. It can be served with steamed baby new potatoes, carrots, broccoli, cauliflower or beans.

Beat the softened butter until smooth. Add the crushed garlic, chopped herbs, lemon juice and pepper and beat well until combined. Wrap the herb butter in greaseproof paper and shape into a roll. Refrigerate until firm. Serve cut into thin slices.

Serves 6

Chinese egg fried rice

This makes a very good accompaniment to stir-fried vegetables or tofu dishes.

Long grain brown rice 8 oz (225 g)
Oil 3 tbsp (45 ml)
Eggs, beaten 2
Large onion, thinly sliced 1
Garlic clove, crushed 1
Small fresh chilli, deseeded & finely chopped 1
Spring onions, thinly sliced diagonally 6
Soya sauce 2 tbsp (30 ml)
Salt & pepper to taste
Spring onion curl to garnish (*see page 237*)

Preparation time: 30 minutes
Cooking time: 45 minutes

Cook the rice in boiling water for 30–40 minutes until just tender. While the rice is cooking, heat 1 tablespoon (15 ml) of the oil in a medium-sized frying pan. Add the beaten eggs, swirling them around to coat the base of the pan. Cook over a medium heat until the eggs are set. Remove from the pan and cut into ½" (1.5 cm) strips. Add the remaining oil to the pan and when hot add the thinly sliced onion. Cook gently until golden brown. Stir the onions throughout cooking to prevent them from burning. Add the garlic, chilli and the sliced spring onions. Cook for 1 minute. Stir in the drained rice, then add the soya sauce and salt and pepper to taste and mix well. Carefully fold in the egg strips. Spoon on to a heated serving dish and garnish with a spring onion curl.

Serves 4

Spiced savoury rice

Butter or margarine 2 oz (50 g)
Onion, chopped 1
Cumin seeds ½ tsp (2.5 ml)
Cardamom pods, crushed 3
Turmeric, ground 1 tsp (5 ml)
Garlic clove, crushed 1
Long grain brown rice 8 oz (225 g)
Vegetable stock 13 fl oz (375 ml)
Cinnamon stick 1" (2.5 cm)
Salt & pepper to taste
Toasted flaked almonds (*see page 20*) 1 oz (25 g)
Fresh coriander (optional)

Preparation time: 20 minutes
Cooking time: 45 minutes

Heat the butter in a heavy-based saucepan, add the finely chopped onion and cook until transparent. Stir in the cumin seeds, cardamom pods, turmeric and crushed garlic. Cook for a minute, then stir in the rice. Add the stock and cinnamon stick. Cover the pan and simmer for about 40 minutes until the rice is tender. Check the rice towards the end of the cooking and, if necessary, add a little more stock. Add salt and pepper to taste. Stir in the almonds and chopped coriander leaves and serve at once.

Serves 3–4

Puddings
& Desserts

Coffee hazelnut meringue

These meringue layers can be made well in advance and stored in an airtight tin. Sandwich together on the day of serving.

Egg whites 6
Raw brown sugar 6 oz (175 g)
Shelled hazelnuts, roasted & ground (*see page 20*)
   4 oz (100 g)
Whipping cream ½ pt (300 ml)
Instant coffee powder 1 tbsp (15 ml)
Boiling water 1 tsp (5 ml)
Grated carob, or fresh fruit (raspberries, strawberries, peaches or nectarines) to decorate

Preparation time: 45 minutes + chilling
Cooking time: 1½ hours

Whisk the egg whites until soft peaks form. Then gradually beat in the sugar, a tablespoonful at a time. Continue to beat until very thick and glossy. Fold in the ground hazelnuts. Divide the mixture evenly between three 8″ (20 cm) sandwich tins lined with greased foil or silicone paper, or shape into three 8″ (20 cm) rounds on lined baking trays. Bake in the oven at 150°C (300°F/Mark 1) for 1 hour. Turn the oven off and leave the meringues to cool in the oven.

Add the coffee mixed with the boiling water to the cream and whip until stiff. Sandwich the 3 meringue rounds with cream. Refrigerate the meringue for several hours before serving. Decorate with grated carob or prepared fruit.

Serves 6–8

Blackcurrant cheesecake

This is a quick and easy cheesecake that requires no jelling agent and no baking.

Base
Digestive biscuits, crushed (*see page 226*) 6 oz (175 g)
Butter or margarine, melted 3 oz (75 g)

Filling
Lebnie or low fat skimmed milk cheese 10 oz (280 g)
Raw brown sugar 2 oz (50 g)
Honey 2 tbsp (30 ml)
Blackcurrants, topped & tailed (fresh or frozen)
 4 oz (100 g)
Double cream, lightly whipped 8 fl oz (250 ml)
Fresh blackcurrant sprigs or lemon balm leaves to decorate

Preparation time: 25 minutes + chilling
No cooking required

Mix together the crushed biscuits and melted butter. Press the mixture evenly over the base of an 8″ (20 cm) loose-bottomed tin. Refrigerate while preparing the filling.

Beat together the Lebnie, sugar and honey until smooth. Stir in the blackcurrants. Then fold in the whipped cream. Spoon evenly over the biscuit base. Refrigerate for several hours until firm. Remove from the tin. Decorate with sprigs of fresh blackcurrants or lemon balm leaves.

Serves 6–8

Carob mousse

These individual mousses are always popular for parties. They can be made the day before and chilled until required. Decorate on the day of serving.

Carob bars, chopped 5 oz (150 g)
Brandy (optional) 2 tsp (10 ml)
Eggs, separated 4
Double cream ¼ pt (150 ml)
Extra whipped cream & grated carob to decorate

Preparation time: 25 minutes
Cooking time: 5 minutes

Put the chopped carob into a bowl and place over a pan of gently simmering water. Stir until just melted, being careful not to let the carob get too hot. Remove from the heat and cool slightly. Add the brandy and the egg yolks and beat until smooth. Whip the cream and fold into the carob mixture. Whisk the egg whites until firm peaks form, then fold into the carob mixture. Spoon into 4 individual dishes. Refrigerate until ready to serve. Decorate with whipped cream and grated carob.

Serves 4

Fresh lemon tart

A favourite in our 'Dine and Wine' evening restaurant. The sharp, tangy flavour is refreshing after a rich meal.

Wholemeal shortcrust pastry made with 5 oz (150 g) of
100% wholemeal flour (see page 22)
Butter or margarine 2 oz (50 g)
Raw brown sugar 4 oz (100 g)
Large lemons, rind & juice of 2

Eggs, beaten 3
Sugared lemon slices (*see below*) to decorate

Preparation time: 30 minutes
Cooking time: about 50 minutes

Sugared lemon slices
Lemon 1
Raw demerara sugar 2 oz (50 g)
Water ¼ pt (150 ml)

Cooking time: 10–15 minutes

Roll out the pastry and use to line a 7½" (19 cm) fluted flan ring. Bake 'blind' at 200°C (400°F/Mark 6) for 10–15 minutes until golden. Put the butter, sugar, lemon rind and juice in a bowl over a pan of simmering water. Stir until the butter has melted and the sugar dissolved. Remove from the heat and stir in the beaten eggs. Pour into the pastry case. Bake in the oven at 180°C (350°F/Mark 4) for about 20–30 minutes until the filling has set. Cool. Decorate with Sugared lemon slices. Serve warm or cold, with pouring cream if wished.

Sugared lemon slices
Cut a thin-skinned lemon into 8 even slices. Place in a frying pan and just cover with water. Bring to the boil. Drain. Dissolve 2 oz (50 g) of raw demerara sugar in ¼ pint (150 ml) water. Bring to the boil, add the lemon slices and boil gently until all the syrup has been absorbed. Cool in the pan.

Serves 4–6

Fresh fruit shortcake

This rich shortcake base is the perfect contrast for the fresh fruit topping. Don't add the fruit too soon or the pastry will go soggy.

Base
100% wholemeal flour 4 oz (100 g)
Butter or margarine 3 oz (75 g)
Egg yolk 1
Raw brown sugar 1 oz (25 g)
Vanilla essence ¼ tsp (1.25 ml)

Topping
Raw sugar apricot jam 3 tbsp (45 ml)
Water 1 tbsp (15 ml)
Fruit in season (strawberries, raspberries, grapes, peaches)
  about 1 lb (450 g)

Preparation time: 30 minutes + chilling
Cooking time: 15–20 minutes

Place the flour in a mixing bowl. Make a well in the centre and add the softened butter, egg yolk, sugar and vanilla. Work to a smooth paste with the finger tips of one hand, drawing in the flour gradually until it makes a smooth dough. Cover and chill for 30 minutes. Press or roll out the pastry to an 8″ (20 cm) round and slide it on to a baking sheet. Flute the edge to give a decorative effect. Bake in the oven at 190°C (375°F/Mark 5) for 15–20 minutes until pale biscuit coloured. Cool.

Put the jam and water in a small saucepan and stir over a low heat until combined. Then sieve a little of the glaze over the cold pastry base. Cover with the prepared fruit, using either one fruit or a mixture. Brush the fruit with the remaining glaze. Serve with soured or whipped cream.

Serves 4–6

Cranks raw sugar brûlée

One of the most delicious desserts ever . . . but plan it two days in advance!

Egg yolks 6
Raw demerara sugar 4 tbsp (60 ml)
Vanilla essence ½ tsp (2.5 ml)
Single cream 1 pt (600 ml)
Raw brown sugar to cover

Preparation time: 30 minutes + refrigerating overnight
Cooking time: 1–1¼ hours

Put the egg yolks, demerara sugar and vanilla into a bowl and beat until pale and thick. Place the cream in a saucepan and stir over the heat until it *almost* boils. Remove from the heat and add to the egg yolk mixture. Beat well with a wooden spoon until combined. Put the bowl over a pan of simmering water and stir until the mixture coats the back of a wooden spoon. Remove from the heat immediately. Strain into 6 individual heatproof dishes. Put the dishes into a baking dish and pour in enough boiling water to come halfway up the sides. Bake in the oven at 150°C (300°F/Mark 2) for about 30 minutes or until the custard has set slightly. Cool. Then refrigerate overnight.

Sift the raw brown sugar and spoon over the custards in a thin even layer. Preheat the grill until very hot. Put the dishes of custard underneath and allow the sugar to melt and brown – be careful not to let it burn. Cool and refrigerate until ready to serve, when it will be deliciously crisp on top and creamy inside.

Alternative
If wished the single cream may be infused with a flavouring before the custard is made. Leave out the vanilla and choose from – a fresh bayleaf, a sprig of fresh rosemary, a few pieces of chopped orange or lemon rind; or add a few drops of rose water or a few drops of orange flower water.

Serves 6

Chilled carob charlotte

A party centrepiece which can be made 2–3 days in advance. Unmould and decorate on the day of serving.

Sponge fingers (see page 207) 16–20
Water 3 tbsp (45 ml)
Brandy 3 tbsp (45 ml)
Eggs, separated 6
Raw brown sugar 4 oz (100 g)
Carob bar, melted 10 oz (300 g)
Instant coffee powder 1 tbsp (15 ml)
Boiling water 1 tsp (5 ml)
Butter or margarine 6 oz (175 g)
Double or whipping cream, lightly whipped ¼ pt (150 ml)
Carob flakes or carob leaves, to decorate (see page 239)

Preparation time: 40 minutes + chilling overnight
Cooking time: 5 minutes

Brush the sponge fingers with the combined water and brandy then use them to line a 2 pt (1.2 l) basin.

Beat the egg yolks and sugar, if possible with an electric mixer, until pale and thick. Mix in the melted carob and the coffee which has been dissolved in the boiling water. Gradually beat in the softened butter. Then fold in the stiffly beaten egg whites. Spoon the mixture into the sponge-lined basin. Cover with cling film and refrigerate overnight.

When ready to serve unmould on to a plate and decorate with whipped cream and carob flakes, or carob leaves.

Serves 8–10

Continental apple slice

A classic combination of ingredients given a different interpretation. Make this on the day of serving.

Digestive biscuits, crushed (*see page 226*) 6 oz (175 g)
Butter or margarine 3½ oz (90 g)
Large cooking apple 1
Sultanas 2 oz (50 g)
Soured cream ½ pt (300 ml)
Raw brown sugar 2 oz (50 g)
Egg yolks 3
Ground mixed spice ½ tsp (2.5 ml)
Grated lemon rind ½ tsp (2.5 ml)

Preparation time: 30 minutes
Cooking time: about 35 minutes

Melt 3 oz (75 g) of the butter and mix well with the biscuit crumbs. Press on to the base of an 8″ (20 cm) round, loose-based tin. Refrigerate until firm.

Wash the apple and core and slice it thinly. Put the sliced apple into a small pan with the remaining butter. Cook, covered, very gently until the apple is just tender, shaking the pan occasionally to prevent sticking. Cool. Arrange the apple and sultanas over the biscuit base.

Beat together the soured cream, half the sugar, egg yolks, spice and lemon rind and pour over the apples. Place the tin on a baking sheet and bake in the oven at 200°C (400°F/ Mark 6) for 15 minutes. Remove from the oven and sieve the remaining sugar evenly over the top. Return to the oven and bake for a further 15 minutes, or until the filling has set. Serve warm or cold.

Serves 6–8

Tropical bananas

This is a very good, easy sweet to make.

Bananas 6
Raw brown sugar 1 oz (25 g)

Orange, rind & juice of 1
Ground cinnamon ¼ tsp (1.25 ml)
Ground nutmeg ¼ tsp (1.25 ml)
Sherry 3 fl oz (75 ml)
Shredded coconut, toasted (optional) (*see page 20*)
2 tbsp (30 ml)

Preparation time: 15 minutes
Cooking time: 15 minutes

Peel the bananas, slice them diagonally and put them into a flat, ovenproof dish. Mix together the sugar, orange rind and juice, spices and sherry in a saucepan. Heat and then pour the mixture over the bananas. Bake in the oven at 190°C (375°F/Mark 5) for about 15 minutes, spooning the juice over the bananas from time to time. Sprinkle with the coconut. Serve with pouring cream, or ice cream, if wished.

Alternative
Use peeled and thinly sliced oranges instead of bananas.

Serves 6

Poached peaches with summer fruit sauce

A perfect way to end a special summer meal. As an alternative leave out the custard filling and just serve the peaches with the fruit sauce.

Custard filling
Egg yolks 2
Raw brown sugar 2 tbsp (30 ml)
Vanilla essence, few drops
Arrowroot 1 tbsp (15 ml)

Milk 8 fl oz (250 ml)
Double cream, lightly whipped ¼ pt (150 ml)

Summer fruit sauce
Redcurrants or blackcurrants 6 oz (175 g)
Strawberries 6 oz (175 g)
Raspberries 6 oz (175 g)
Honey or raw brown sugar to taste

Poached peaches
Water 2 pts (1.2 l)
Lemon, grated rind of 1
Honey 2 tbsp (30 ml)
Peaches 6
Mint sprigs to decorate

Preparation time: about 45 minutes + cooling
Cooking time: about 30 minutes

Custard filling

Beat the egg yolks, sugar, vanilla and arrowroot until smooth. Heat the milk until it just boils. Pour on to the egg yolk mixture and stir until smooth. Return to the saucepan and stir over a low heat until the custard boils and thickens. Remove from the heat immediately and beat with a wooden spoon until smooth. Strain. When completely cold fold in the whipped cream.

Summer fruit sauce

Wash the fruit, remove the stalks from the currants and hull and slice the strawberries. Put the fruit into a saucepan and cook over a medium heat until the juices just begin to run, stirring occasionally. Taste and, if necessary, sweeten with a little honey or raw sugar. Cool. Purée if wished and sieve to remove seeds.

Poached peaches

Combine the water, lemon rind and honey in a saucepan large enough to hold the peaches in one layer. Bring to the boil. Carefully drop in the peaches and simmer gently for 5 minutes. Remove from the heat and allow to cool in the liquid. Peel off the skins, cut the peaches in half and remove the stones.

Spoon a little of the fruit sauce into the base of 6 individual serving dishes. Place the peach halves cut side up on top of the sauce. Spoon a little of the custard into the hollows of each peach. Decorate with tiny mint sprigs.

Serves 6

Strawberry coconut flan

Base
Ground almonds 4 oz (100 g)
Shredded coconut 4 oz (100 g)
Raw brown sugar 1 oz (25 g)
Butter or margarine, melted 2 oz (50 g)

Filling
Cream cheese or low fat skimmed milk cheese 8 oz (225 g)
Soured cream 2 tbsp (30 ml)
Raw brown sugar 1 oz (25 g)
Small lemon, grated rind of 1
Lemon juice 1 tsp (5 ml)
Strawberries 8 oz (225 g)
Raw sugar strawberry jam 4 tbsp (60 ml)

Preparation time: 35 minutes + chilling
Cooking time: 15 minutes

Mix together the almonds, coconut, sugar and melted butter. Press the mixture firmly on to the base and sides of a well greased 8″ (20 cm) fluted flan tin. Bake in the oven at 190°C (375°F/Mark 5) for 12–15 minutes until pale golden brown. Watch it carefully as it will burn very easily. Cool.

Beat the softened cream cheese, soured cream, sugar, lemon

rind and juice together until smooth. Spread evenly over the coconut base. Hull and slice the strawberries (keeping 1 whole with its leaves for decoration). Arrange them over the top of the flan. Put the jam into a small bowl and place it over a pan of simmering water until warm. Sieve. Then brush the jam over the strawberries to glaze. Decorate.

Serves 6–8

Baked lemon cheesecake

Biscuit base
Digestive biscuits (*see page 226*) 6 oz (175 g)
Butter or margarine 3 oz (75 g)

Filling
Cream cheese or low fat skimmed milk cheese
  12 oz (350 g)
Raw brown sugar 3 oz (75 g)
Eggs, separated 3
Soured cream 8 fl oz (250 ml)
Large lemon, grated rind of 1
Lemon juice 1 tbsp (15 ml)
Salt (optional), pinch
Whipped cream & fresh fruit to decorate

Preparation time: 30 minutes
Cooking time: 40–50 minutes

Finely crush the biscuits, stir in the melted butter and mix well. Press into the base of an 8″ (20 cm) loose-bottomed deep cake tin which has been lined with greaseproof paper. Refrigerate while preparing the filling.

Put the cream cheese, sugar, egg yolks, soured cream, lemon rind and juice into a basin and beat until completely smooth. Whip the egg whites and salt until soft peaks form. Then fold into the cream cheese mixture. Spread over the biscuit base. Bake in the oven at 180°C (350°F/Mark 4) for

40–50 minutes or until the filling is set. Cool. (As the cheesecake cools cracks may appear in the filling, but this is quite usual if the cheesecake is baked.)

Decorate if wished with whipped cream and fresh fruit – strawberries, grapes, or peeled and sliced kiwi fruit.

Serves 4–6

Pecan pie

This has been adapted from the traditional American recipe and is a real favourite at Cranks.

100% wholemeal shortcrust pastry made with 6 oz (175 g) of flour (*see page 22*)
Pecan nuts, shelled 6 oz (175 g)
Butter or margarine 4 oz (100 g)
Thick honey 8 oz (225 g)
Molasses 3 oz (75 g)
Raw brown sugar 1 oz (25 g)
Eggs 3
Vanilla essence 1 tsp (5 ml)
Lemon, grated rind of 1
Brandy 1 tsp (5 ml)
Ground nutmeg 1 tsp (5 ml)

Preparation time: 25 minutes
Cooking time: 50–55 minutes

Roll out the pastry and use to line a 9″ (23 cm) fluted flan tin. Bake 'blind' in the oven at 200°C (400°F/Mark 6) for 10–15 minutes until pale golden. Lightly roast 4 oz (100 g) pecan nuts on a baking tray in the oven at the same time, for about 15 minutes, giving them an occasional stir. Leave to cool and then chop them.

Beat the butter, honey, molasses and sugar together until light and fluffy. Add the eggs, one at a time, beating well after each addition. Then add the vanilla, lemon rind, brandy and nutmeg and beat well. Mix in the chopped pecan nuts. Pour the mixture into the pastry case. Decorate with the remaining pecan nuts. Bake in the oven at 160°C (325°F/ Mark 3) for 40–45 minutes, or until the filling has set. Serve warm with cream or soured cream.

Serves 8

Lemon mousse

Unsalted butter 3 oz (75 g)
Lemons, rind & juice of 2
Raw brown sugar 2 oz (50 g)
Eggs, beaten 3
Double cream, whipped ¼ pt (150 ml)
Egg whites 2
Fresh lemon slices to decorate

Preparation time: 20 minutes + cooling
Cooking time: 20–30 minutes

Put the butter, lemon rind and juice and sugar into a bowl over gently simmering water. Allow the butter to melt. Add the beaten eggs to the lemon mixture and stir until the mixture thickens and coats the back of a wooden spoon – about 20–30 minutes. Cool. Fold in the whipped cream. Stiffly whisk the egg whites and fold into the lemon mixture. Spoon into serving dishes and chill until required. Decorate with twists of fresh lemon.

Serves 4

Poached plums with cinnamon cream

This simple dessert looks lovely served in a glass dish. It is ideal for a buffet party.

Red wine ¼ pt (150 ml)
Raw sugar plum or raspberry jam 2 tbsp (30 ml)
Orange, grated rind & juice of 1
Plums, stoned & halved 2 lb (900 g)

Cinnamon cream
Double cream ¼ pt (150 ml)
Honey 1 tsp (5 ml)
Ground cinnamon ½ tsp (2.5 ml)

Preparation time: 15 minutes
Cooking time: about 10 minutes

Put the wine, jam, orange rind and juice into a medium-sized saucepan. Bring to the boil. Then add the plums. Cover the pan and simmer gently for 5–10 minutes until just tender. Cool. Refrigerate until ready to serve. Serve with Cinnamon cream.

Cinnamon cream
Mix the cream, honey and cinnamon together in a basin and beat lightly until thickened.

Serves 4

Apple & hazelnut lattice pie

A very special version of the traditional English apple pie.

Hazelnut pastry
100% wholemeal flour 6 oz (175 g)
Ground cinnamon 1 tsp (5 ml)
Raw brown sugar 2 oz (50 g)

Lemon, grated rind of 1
Unsalted butter or margarine 4 oz (100 g)
Shelled hazelnuts, roasted & ground (*see page 20*)
    3 oz (75 g)
Egg yolks 2
Vanilla essence 1 tsp (5 ml)
Water 2 tsp (10 ml)
Glaze (optional) mix 1 egg yolk with 2 tsp (10 ml) soured
    cream or milk

Apple filling
Medium-sized cooking apples 2
Water 1 tbsp (15 ml)
Sultanas 2 oz (50 g)

Preparation time: 30–35 minutes + chilling
Cooking time: about 40 minutes

Put the flour, cinnamon, sugar and lemon rind into a mixing bowl, or food processor. Add the softened butter cut into small pieces and rub into the flour. Add the hazelnuts, egg yolks, vanilla and 2 teaspoons (10 ml) water. Mix to a firm dough and refrigerate until firm enough to handle – approximately 20 minutes.

Wipe, core and slice the apples. Put them into a saucepan with the water and cook gently, covered, until just tender. Do not allow the apple to become pulpy. Add the sultanas. Cool.

Press two-thirds of the hazelnut pastry into an 8" (20 cm) pie plate. Spread the apple filling over the pastry. Roll out the remaining pastry to a rectangle about 8" × 5" (20 × 15 cm) and cut into ½" (1.5 cm) strips. Arrange in a lattice over the apple filling, pressing the ends of the strips to the rim to secure them. Trim the edges. To give the pie a rich glaze, brush with combined egg yolk and soured cream. Bake in the oven at 190°C (375°F/Mark 5) for 30 minutes or until golden brown. Serve warm.

Serves 6–8

Winter fruit salad

Dried apricots, washed 4 oz (100 g)
Prunes, washed 4 oz (100 g)
Currants 2 oz (50 g)
Unsweetened white grape juice ½ pt (300 ml)
Water ¼ pt (150 ml)
Clear honey 2 tbsp (30 ml)
Dessert apple, cored & diced 1
Pear, cored & diced 1
Pineapple, peeled and diced 4 oz (100 g)
Oranges 2
Large banana, peeled 1

Preparation time: 20 minutes + cooling
Cooking time: 20 minutes

Place the first 6 ingredients in a saucepan and bring to the boil. Reduce the heat, cover and simmer for 15 minutes. Leave to cool. Add the apple, pear and pineapple. Using a serrated knife, peel the oranges, collecting any juice, and cut into bite-size pieces. Lastly chop the banana and mix all the fruit together.

Serves 6–8

Fresh fruit salad

Unsweetened white grape juice ¼ pt (150 ml)
Clear honey 2 tbsp (30 ml)
Seedless grapes 4 oz (100 g)
Strawberries 4 oz (100 g)
Dessert apple, cored 1
Pear, cored 1
Orange 1

Banana, peeled 1
Kiwi fruit, peeled 1
Melon, peeled & diced 4 oz (100 g)
Pineapple, peeled & diced 4 oz (100 g)

Preparation time: about 25 minutes

Mix the grape juice and honey together in a large bowl.
Halve the grapes, hull and slice or halve the strawberries.
Chop the apple and pear. Add to the juice. Using a serrated
knife, peel the orange, collecting any juice, and cut into bite-
size pieces. Slice the banana and kiwi fruit. Add the melon
and pineapple. Mix all the fruit together. Decorate, if possible, with fresh borage flowers.

Serves 6–8

Brandied caramel oranges

*It is essential to choose really good quality, thin skinned oranges
for this recipe.*

Large oranges 4
Raw demerara sugar 4 oz (100 g)
Cold water 3 fl oz (75 ml)
Warm water 2 fl oz (50 ml)
Brandy 2 tbsp (30 ml)

Preparation time: about 45 minutes + chilling
Cooking time: about 30 minutes

Using a vegetable peeler, remove strips of peel from 1 of the
oranges, being careful not to include any of the white pith.
Cut the peel into very fine shreds and cover with a little
boiling water. Using a serrated knife, cut the rind and pith
from the oranges. Hold each orange over a plate while

working to catch the juice. Cut each orange into thin slices, then reshape the slices, securing them with a wooden cocktail stick, so that they look like complete oranges.

Put the sugar and cold water into a pan over a very gentle heat. Shake the pan gently until the sugar has dissolved. Then allow to boil steadily until it becomes a thick syrup. Boil a little longer until it turns a rich caramel, being careful not to let it burn. Remove from the heat. Carefully pour in the warm water. Return the pan to a gentle heat to dissolve the caramel. Off the heat, stir the reserved orange juice into the caramel sauce and add the brandy.

Put the oranges into a dish just large enough to hold them. Cover with the caramel sauce, sprinkle with the strained orange shreds and refrigerate for several hours, or overnight, to allow the oranges to absorb the flavour.

Serves 4

Fruit mince flan

This recipe is particularly good – and seasonal at Christmas time. The fruit mince filling will keep for up to a month in the refrigerator.

Wholemeal shortcrust pastry made with 8 oz (225 g) of 100% wholemeal flour (*see page 22*)
Fruit mince filling (*see below*) 1 lb (450 g)
Beaten egg to glaze
Raw demerara sugar (optional) to sprinkle

Preparation time: 25 minutes
Cooking time: about 30 minutes

Fruit mince filling
Cooking apple, cored & finely chopped 4 oz (100 g)
Nutter 1 oz (25 g)

Raisins 3 oz (75 g)
Sultanas 3 oz (75 g)
Currants 3 oz (75 g)
Raw brown sugar 2 oz (50 g)
Ground cinnamon ¼ tsp (1.25 ml)
Ground nutmeg ¼ tsp (1.25 ml)
Ground mixed spice ¼ tsp (1.25 ml)
Orange, grated rind & juice of ½
Lemon, grated rind & juice of ½
Flaked almonds ½ oz (12.5 g)
Brandy 1–2 tbsp (15–30 ml)

Preparation time: 15 minutes
Cooking time: about 2 hours

Roll out just over half the pastry on a lightly floured surface and use it to line an 8″ (20 cm) fluted flan tin. Spoon in the fruit mince and level the surface. Roll out the remaining pastry to a rectangle about 8″ (20 cm) by 5″ (15 cm) and cut it into ½″ (1.5 cm) strips. Brush the rim of the flan with a little beaten egg. Arrange the strips of pastry in a lattice over the fruit mince. Trim the edges, then brush the lattice with the beaten egg. Sprinkle the top lightly with raw demerara sugar. Bake in the oven at 200°C (400°F/Mark 6) for approximately 30 minutes, or until golden brown. Serve warm.

Serves 6

Fruit mince filling

Put all the ingredients, except the almonds and brandy, into a deep ovenproof dish and mix together thoroughly. Cover with a lid or foil and bake in the oven at 120°C (250°F/Mark ½) for 1 hour. Give the mincemeat a good stir halfway through the cooking time. Then leave it to cool before adding the almonds and brandy. Keep refrigerated.

Makes about 1 lb (450 g)

Strawberry trifle

Sponge
Butter or margarine 3½ oz (90 g)
Raw brown sugar 3½ oz (90 g)
Eggs 2
100% wholemeal flour 3½ oz (90 g)
Baking powder 1 tsp (5 ml)
or
Left-over plain cake 12 oz–1 lb (350–450 g)

Custard
Milk ¾ pt (450 ml)
Egg yolks 3
Raw brown sugar 2 tbsp (30 ml)
Vanilla essence ½ tsp (2.5 ml)
Arrowroot 1 tbsp (15 ml)
Whipping cream ½ pt (300 ml)

Sherry to taste
Strawberries 12 oz (350 g)

Preparation time: 30 minutes
Cooking time: 30 minutes

Beat the butter and sugar together until light and creamy.
Then gradually add the eggs, beating well after each addition.
Fold in the combined flour and baking powder. Spread the
mixture into a 7″ (18 cm) sandwich tin lined with greased,
greaseproof paper. Bake in the oven at 180°C (350°F/Mark 4)
for about 20–25 minutes until just firm to the touch. Cool
slightly in the tin then turn out on to a wire rack.

Put the milk into a small saucepan and bring to the boil.
Beat the egg yolks, sugar, vanilla and arrowroot until smooth.
Beat in the milk. Return to the saucepan and stir over a low
heat until the mixture just boils and thickens. Remove from
the heat immediately. Cool. Fold in approximately half of the
whipped cream.

Break the cake into pieces and put it into the base of a

serving dish, or 6 individual dishes. Sprinkle generously with sherry to moisten. Keep 6 strawberries for decoration, slice the remainder and arrange over the sponge. Spoon the custard on top. Decorate with the remaining whipped cream and strawberries.

Serves 6–8

Rhubarb fool

The age-old favourite but always a winner if made correctly.

Rhubarb 12 oz (350 g)
Raw brown sugar 1 tbsp (15 ml)

Custard
Single cream and/or milk ¾ pt (450 ml)
Egg yolks 3
Raw brown sugar 1½ tbsp (25 ml)
Arrowroot 1 tbsp (15 ml)
Vanilla essence ¼ tsp (1.25 ml)

Preparation time: 25 minutes + chilling
Cooking time: about 20 minutes

Wash and slice the rhubarb, put it into a saucepan and sprinkle with the sugar. Cook over a gentle heat until the rhubarb is pulpy and thick, stirring occasionally – about 10–15 minutes. Chill.

Put the cream or milk into a saucepan and heat until boiling. Beat the egg yolks, sugar, arrowroot and vanilla until combined. Then whisk in the boiling milk and return to the saucepan. Continue to whisk over the heat until the mixture becomes thick. Remove from the heat immediately. Cool. Mix the rhubarb and the custard together and spoon into individual glasses. Chill until required.

Alternatives

Rhubarb with blackcurrant fool Use 8 oz (225 g) of rhubarb and cook as above. Then while still hot stir in 4 oz (100 g) of frozen blackcurrants. Chill.

Mango fool Peel and remove the flesh from 2 medium-sized mangoes, and purée – there should be about 8 fl oz (250 ml). Continue as main recipe using mango instead of rhubarb.

Serves 6

Apricot & almond crumble

Fresh apricots are truly delicious in this pudding, but if you want to make it out of season dried apricots can be substituted.

Fresh apricots 2 lb (900 g) or dried apricots (*see page 182*) 12 oz (350 g)
Water 3 tbsp (45 ml)
Honey to taste

Crumble
100% wholemeal flour 3 oz (75 g)
Rolled oats 2 oz (50 g)
Flaked almonds 2 oz (50 g)
Raw brown sugar 2–3 oz (50–75 g)
Butter or margarine, melted 3 oz (75 g)

Preparation time: 15 minutes
Cooking time: 30–35 minutes

Wash, halve and stone the apricots. Put them into a pan with the water, cover, and cook very gently until just tender – 5–10 minutes. If necessary sweeten with a little honey. Spoon into a 1½ pt (900 ml) pie dish.

Mix together the flour, oats, almonds, sugar and melted butter. Sprinkle evenly over the fruit, pressing the crumble down very lightly. Bake in the oven at 180°C (350°F/Mark 4) for about 30 minutes until golden.

Dried apricots Put 12 oz (350 g) apricots into boiling water and soak for 4–6 hours. Drain, reserving the liquid. Put the apricots into a saucepan with 3 tablespoons of juice and 1 tablespoon of honey. Simmer for 2–3 minutes.

Serves 6

Summer pudding

There is such a short period when one can make this lovely pudding using all the fresh summer berries – do take advantage of it!

Red summer fruits (strawberries, redcurrants,
   blackcurrants, raspberries, cherries) 2 lb (900 g)
Raw brown sugar 1 oz (25 g)
100% wholemeal bread 8–10 slices
Fresh redcurrants & leaves to decorate

Preparation time: 30 minutes + chilling overnight
Cooking time: 5 minutes

Wash the fruit, hull and slice the strawberries, remove the stalks from the currants and stone the cherries. Put all the fruit in a pan and sprinkle with the sugar. Cook over a medium heat for 3–5 minutes, stirring occasionally, until the sugar dissolves. Remove from the heat.

Remove the crusts from the bread and use the slices to line a buttered 2 pt (900 ml) pudding basin. Press the edges together firmly and fill in any gaps with small pieces of bread. Using a slotted spoon fill the basin with the fruit. Reserve the juices that are left behind. Cover the pudding with the remaining bread. Cover the basin with a small plate and

weight it down with a 2 or 3 lb (900 g or 1.4 kg) weight.
Refrigerate overnight.

Carefully turn the pudding out on to a dish and spoon the
reserved juices over. Decorate with redcurrants.

Serves 6–8

Bread, Rolls
& Toasts

Wholemeal bread, baps & rolls

For a decorative effect, sprinkle loaves or rolls with sesame or poppy seeds before baking. Brush the dough lightly with water or beaten egg to make the seeds stick.

100% wholemeal flour 3 lb (1.35 kg)
Sea salt 1 tbsp (15 ml)
Fresh yeast (or equivalent dried yeast) 1 oz (25 g)
Raw brown sugar 1 tbsp (15 ml)
Water 1½–2 pts (900 ml)

Makes 2 large loaves

100% wholemeal flour 1 lb (450 g)
Sea salt 1 tsp (5 ml)
Fresh yeast (or equivalent dried yeast) ½ oz (15 g)
Raw brown sugar 1 tsp (5 ml)
Water ½–⅔ pt (300–400 ml)

Makes 1 loaf or 6 baps

Preparation time: 30 minutes + 40–60 minutes rising time
Cooking time:
  loaves: 35–40 minutes
  baps: 20–25 minutes
  rolls: 15–20 minutes

Mix the flour with the salt (in very cold weather warm the flour slightly, enough to take the chill off). Mix the yeast and sugar in a small bowl, with ¼ pt (150 ml) of the warm water.

Leave in a warm place for 10–20 minutes to froth. Pour the yeast liquid into the flour and gradually add sufficient water to make a soft manageable dough. Knead well to give a smooth dough. Divide the dough between two 2 pt (900 ml) bread tins (round cake tins may be used instead) which have been greased and warmed. Put the tins in a warm place, cover with a cloth or oiled polythene, and leave for 30–40 minutes to rise, or until the dough is within ½″ (1 cm) of the top of the tins. Bake in the oven at 200°C (400°F/Mark 6) for about 35–40 minutes. Allow to cool for a few minutes and turn out on to a wire tray.

Baps
Roll out the dough thickly on a lightly floured surface and stamp out six 4″ (10 cm) rounds. Place on a baking sheet, brush lightly with milk and leave in a warm place to prove for 10–15 minutes. Bake in the oven at 200°C (400°F/Mark 6) for 20–25 minutes. Cool on a wire tray.

Rolls
Shape the dough into rolls and leave to rise until doubled in size. Then bake for 15–20 minutes until they sound hollow when tapped on the base.

Cranks crescents

It's best to start these the day before you need them and chill the dough overnight.

100% wholemeal flour 12 oz (350 g)
Salt, large pinch
Butter or margarine at room temperature 8 oz (225 g)
Fresh yeast ½ oz (15 g)
Milk, lukewarm 8 fl oz (250 ml)
Beaten egg to glaze

Preparation time: about 50 minutes + chilling overnight
Cooking time: 20–25 minutes

Combine the flour and salt in a basin. Rub in 2 oz (50 g) of the butter. Cream the yeast in a bowl with the lukewarm milk. Make a well in the centre of the flour and pour in the yeast mixture. Mix with a knife to give a soft dough. Turn on to a lightly floured board and knead for 10 minutes. Roll out the dough into a rectangle 3 times as long as it is wide. Dot the top two-thirds of the dough with half the butter. Fold the dough in three, folding the unbuttered third up, then the buttered top third down and pressing the edges to seal them. Give a 90° clockwise turn so that the folded closed edge is to your right. Roll out again into a rectangle. Dot the top two-thirds with the remaining butter. Fold, turn and roll again. Fold, then wrap loosely in a plastic bag. Refrigerate for 1 hour. Roll and fold twice more. Leave in the refrigerator for several hours, preferably overnight.

Divide the dough in half. Roll each piece into a square measuring approximately 10″ (25 cm). Cut into 4 even-sized squares. Roll up each square of dough starting at one corner and roll to the opposite corner. Shape into a horseshoe shape. Place on a lightly greased tray and stand in a warm place until doubled in size. Brush with lightly beaten egg and bake in the oven at 200°C (400°F/Mark 6) for 20–25 minutes until golden.

Makes 8

Continental fruit plait

A rich dough shaped into an attractive plait with a spiced apple filling. Perfect with coffee.

Dough
100% wholemeal flour 1 lb (450 g)

Salt, large pinch
Milk, lukewarm 6 fl oz (175 g)
Fresh yeast ½ oz (15 g)
Butter or margarine, melted 2 oz (50 g)
Raw brown sugar 2 oz (50 g)
Eggs, lightly beaten 2
Clear honey to glaze

Filling
Large cooking apple, cored & finely chopped 1
Sultanas 8 oz (225 g)
Raw brown sugar 1 oz (25 g)
Butter or margarine 1 oz (25 g)
Ground cinnamon 1 tsp (5 ml)
Flaked almonds 1 oz (25 g)

Preparation time: 30–40 minutes + 1½ hours rising time
Cooking time: 30–40 minutes

Combine the flour and salt in a large basin and make a well in the centre. Mix together the lukewarm milk, yeast, melted butter, sugar and lightly beaten eggs and pour into the flour. Mix to a smooth dough, first using a wooden spoon, then using your hand. Knead the dough until smooth and elastic – about 5 minutes. Put the dough into a clean basin, brush the top with oil and cover with polythene. Leave in a warm place until doubled in bulk, approximately 1 hour. Knead lightly, then roll out on a lightly floured surface to an oblong 8″ × 15″ (20 cm × 48 cm). Spread the filling down the middle of the dough. Make cuts in the dough at either side of the filling at 1″ (2.5 cm) intervals. Lift a strip from each side alternately and cross one over the other to form a plait. Tuck the ends neatly underneath the plait. Lift on to a lightly greased baking tray. Brush the top lightly with oil, cover with polythene and leave to rise in a warm place for 30 minutes until puffy. Bake in the oven at 200°C (400°F/Mark 6) for 30–40 minutes. While still warm, brush with honey.

Filling
Put the finely chopped apples, sultanas, sugar and butter into

a small saucepan. Cover and cook very gently until the apple is tender – about 10 minutes. Cool. Then stir in the cinnamon and almonds.

Wholemeal crumpets

Quite simple to prepare, if a little time-consuming, these crumpets are delicious and well worth the effort.

100% wholemeal flour 1¼ lb (575 g)
Baking powder 2 tbsp (30 ml)
Salt 1 tsp (5 ml)
Fresh yeast ½ oz (15 g)
Raw brown sugar 1 tsp (5 ml)
Water, lukewarm 1½ pts (900 ml)

Preparation time: 30 minutes + 1 hour rising time
Cooking time: 15 minutes

Combine the flour, baking powder and salt in a large bowl. Mix together the yeast, sugar and a ¼ pt (150 ml) of the lukewarm water. Leave to rest in a warm place until frothy – approximately 10 minutes. Add the yeast mixture and the remaining 1¼ pts (750 ml) of lukewarm water to the dry ingredients and beat until smooth. Leave to stand in a warm place for 45 minutes.

Lightly grease some crumpet rings, egg poaching rings, or use large pastry cutters, and put them into a lightly greased frying pan. Place over a low heat and allow to heat through. Pour about 3 tablespoons of the mixture into each ring. Cook over a low heat for about 10 minutes. Remove the rings and turn the crumpets over. Cook for a further 2–3 minutes. Cool on a wire tray.

Serve either warm, fresh from the pan, or well toasted and spread with butter. Any left over crumpets may be frozen.

Makes about 25

Herbed potato bread

*This is very good for a packed lunch or picnic, or to serve with a
salad main course.*

Fresh yeast 1 oz (25 g)
Raw brown sugar 1 tsp (5 ml)
Milk, lukewarm 10 fl oz (300 ml)
100% wholemeal flour 12 oz (350 g)
Salt 1 tsp (5 ml)
Dried mixed herbs 1 tsp (5 ml)
Spring onions, trimmed & chopped 4
Cheddar cheese, grated 2 oz (50 g)
Potato, cooked & mashed 8 oz (225 g)
Beaten egg to glaze

*Preparation time: about 30 minutes + 1¼ hours rising time
Cooking time: 30–40 minutes*

Cream the yeast with the sugar and half the lukewarm milk
and stand in a warm place for 10–20 minutes until frothy.
Put the flour, salt, herbs, spring onions, cheese and cold
potato into a basin and add the yeast mixture and the
remaining lukewarm milk. Mix well to give a soft dough.
Turn on to a floured board and knead for 5 minutes. Shape
the dough into a loaf and put it into a well greased 9″ × 5″
(23 cm × 12 cm) tin. Brush the top with oil, cover and stand
in a warm place until the dough reaches the top of the tin –
approximately 1 hour. Brush with lightly beaten egg. Bake in
the oven at 200°C (400°F/Mark 6) for 30–40 minutes or until
the bread sounds hollow when tapped on the base.

Makes 1 loaf

Pitta bread

*Serve warm with Chick pea or Aubergine & tahini dips, Tzatziki
or Spiced cauliflower with tomato, or cut a pocket in each pitta
and fill it with mixed salad.*

100% wholemeal flour 2 lb (900 g)
Salt 2 tsp (10 ml)
Fresh yeast ½ oz (15 g)
Raw brown sugar 2 tsp (10 ml)
Water, lukewarm 1–1¼ pts (600–700 ml)

Preparation time: 40 minutes + 1½ hours rising time
Cooking time: 12–15 minutes

Combine the flour and salt in a large basin. Mix the yeast and sugar in a small bowl with ¼ pint (150 ml) of the warm water. Leave in a warm place for 10–20 minutes until frothy. Pour the yeast into the flour and gradually add enough warm water to give a soft but not sticky dough. Cover with polythene and leave to stand for 10 minutes. Knead lightly on a floured surface. Divide the dough into 10 equal portions. Knead each portion lightly, then roll out into an oval, approximately 8″ × 5″ (20 cm × 12 cm). Place the pitta bread on to a lightly floured oven tray. Brush the tops lightly with oil. Then leave to rise in a warm place for about 1 hour. At this stage the pitta should feel quite light and puffy to the touch. Bake in the oven at 240°C (475°F/Mark 9) for 12–15 minutes until golden. As soon as the pitta bread comes out of the oven, brush very lightly with a little water. Cool on a wire tray.

Makes 10

Wholemeal griddle cakes

Originally cooked on a flat, open griddle these are delicious for breakfast with butter and honey, or with scrambled eggs.

100% wholemeal self raising flour 6 oz (175 g)
Baking powder 2 tsp (10 ml)
Salt ½ tsp (2.5 ml)
Raw brown sugar 1 tbsp (15 ml)

Butter or margarine ½ oz (15 g)
Egg 1
Milk ½ pt (300 ml)

Preparation time: 10 minutes
Cooking time: about 20 minutes

Put the flour, baking powder, salt and sugar into a basin. Beat together the butter, egg and milk. Pour the liquid into the flour and beat until smooth. Heat a lightly greased griddle or frying pan and pour approximately 2–3 tablespoons of the batter on to the pan for each cake. Cook until bubbles start to appear on the surface. Then turn and cook until golden on the other side. Repeat with the remaining batter.

Makes about 10

Melba toast

Take care when baking the toast – it should be crisp, but not over baked.

Day-old wholemeal bread

Preparation time: 5–10 minutes
Cooking time: 7–8 minutes

Cut the bread into wafer thin slices with a sharp, serrated knife. Arrange in a single layer on a baking sheet and bake in the oven at 200°C (400°F/Mark 6) for 7–8 minutes until really crisp and golden. Cool on a wire tray. Keep in an airtight container.

Corn bread

Good with chilli bean & Mixed vegetable casserole, or other spiced main dishes.

Cornmeal (unrefined maize flour) 4 oz (100 g)
100% wholemeal flour 4 oz (100 g)
Salt 1 tsp (5 ml)
Baking powder 2 tsp (10 ml)
Eggs, lightly beaten 2
Buttermilk, or milk or soya milk 12 fl oz (350 ml)
Honey 1 tbsp (15 ml)
Oil 3 tbsp (45 ml)

Preparation time: 15 minutes
Cooking time: 30–35 minutes

Mix together the cornmeal, flour, salt and baking powder. Combine the lightly beaten eggs, buttermilk, honey and oil and mix into the dry ingredients. Pour into a greased, greaseproof paper-lined 8″ (20 cm) square tin. Bake in the oven at 220°C (425°F/Mark 7) for 30–35 minutes. Cut into squares and serve while still warm.

Makes 16 squares

Sesame seed knots

100% wholemeal flour 2 lb (900 g)
Salt 2 tsp (10 ml)
Sesame seeds, toasted (*see page 20*) 2 oz (50 g)
Fresh yeast ½ oz (15 g)
Raw brown sugar 2 tsp (10 ml)
Water, lukewarm 1–1¼ pts (600–700 ml)
Oil to glaze
Beaten egg to glaze
Sesame seeds to sprinkle

Preparation time: about 1 hour + 1½ hours rising time
Cooking time: about 25 minutes

Mix together the flour, salt and toasted sesame seeds. Mix the yeast and sugar in a small bowl with ¼ pint (150 ml) of the warm water. Leave in a warm place for 10–20 minutes or until frothy. Pour the yeast mixture into the flour and add enough warm water to give a soft but not sticky dough. Cover with polythene and leave to stand in a warm place for 10 minutes. Knead lightly on a floured surface. Divide the dough into 16 equal portions. Knead each portion into a ball. Then roll each one under the palm of the hand until about 10″ (25 cm) long. Tie into a knot and place on a greased oven tray. Brush the knots lightly with oil. Set aside in a warm place until they have doubled in bulk – about 30 minutes. At this stage they should feel very light when pressed gently with the fingers. Brush the tops of the rolls with the beaten egg and sprinkle with sesame seeds. Bake in the oven at 200°C (400°F/Mark 6) for about 25 minutes. Cool on a wire rack.

Makes 16

Oatmeal & treacle bread

100% wholemeal flour 3 lb (1.4 kg)
Salt 1 tbsp (15 ml)
Porridge oats 6 oz (175 g)
Fresh yeast 1 oz (25 g)
Raw brown sugar 1 tsp (5 ml)
Water, lukewarm 4 tbsp (60 ml)
Milk 1½ pts (900 ml)
Butter or margarine 2 oz (50 g)
Treacle 4 tbsp (60 ml)
Lightly beaten egg, water or milk to glaze
Porridge oats or poppy seeds to sprinkle

Preparation time: about 40 minutes + 1¼ hours rising time
Cooking time: about 40 minutes

Combine the flour, salt and oats in a large bowl. Mix together the yeast, sugar and the lukewarm water and leave it in a warm place until it becomes frothy – 10–20 minutes. Put the milk, butter and treacle into a small pan and stir over a low heat until the butter has melted. Cool until lukewarm. Add the yeast and the milk mixture to the dry ingredients and mix to give a soft dough. Add a little more milk if the mixture seems too dry. Put the dough into a greased basin and cover with polythene. Leave in a warm place for 10 minutes. Then knead it on a lightly floured board until smooth and elastic. Divide the dough into 2 halves and place each portion into a greased 2 lb (900 g) loaf tin. Brush the tops with oil and cover lightly with polythene film. Leave to rise in a warm place until the dough reaches the top of the tins – about 40 minutes. Brush the tops with egg, milk or water and sprinkle with oats or poppy seeds. Bake in the oven at 200°C (400°F/Mark 6) for approximately 40 minutes. Cool on a wire rack.

Makes 2 large loaves

Indian puris

Puri is deep-fried Indian wholewheat bread. Both these Indian breads are best eaten fresh with spiced main dishes.

100% wholemeal flour 8 oz (225 g)
Salt 1 tsp (5 ml)
Butter or margarine 2 oz (50 g)
Water 3 fl oz (75 ml)
Oil for deep frying

Preparation time: 30 minutes + 1 hour rising time
Cooking time: about 20–30 minutes

Combine the flour and salt in a basin and rub in the butter until the mixture resembles fine breadcrumbs. Using a knife, stir in the water to give a pliable dough. Turn on to a lightly floured surface and knead for 10 minutes until smooth and elastic. Cover loosely with polythene and leave to rise in a warm place for 1 hour. Roll out the dough on a lightly floured surface until it is paper thin. Cut into rounds using a 4″ (10 cm) round cutter. Cover the puris with a damp cloth as you cut, to prevent them drying out. Place the puris, one at a time into deep, very hot oil. Using a slotted spoon, gently hold them under the oil until the puri starts to puff. Fry until golden.

Makes about 15

Paratha – Indian layered bread

100% wholemeal flour 12 oz (350 g)
Salt ½ tsp (2.5 ml)
Oil 6 tbsp (90 ml)
Water 7 fl oz (200 ml)
Butter or margarine 2 oz (50 g)

Preparation time: about 1 hour + 30 minutes rising time
Cooking time: about 15 minutes

Put the flour and salt into a basin. Sprinkle in 2 tablespoons (30 ml) of the oil and rub in with the finger tips until the mixture resembles breadcrumbs. Add enough water to give a soft but not sticky dough. Knead until smooth and elastic – about 5 minutes. Form the dough into a ball and brush it with the combined melted butter and remaining 4 tablespoons (60 ml) of oil. Wrap in polythene and set aside for 30 minutes. Divide the dough into 12 even pieces. Work with one piece at a time and keep the remaining dough covered. Roll out the dough into a thin circle on a lightly floured work surface. Brush lightly with the oil and butter. Fold the circle in half

and brush the top of the semicircle with the butter and oil.
Fold in half again to form a triangle. Roll out the dough to
form a large triangle with approximately 7″ (18 cm) sides. Put
a frying pan over a medium heat and when hot, brush with
butter and oil. Put the parathas into the pan, one at a time,
and cook for about a minute, brush the top with butter and
oil and when golden brown turn to cook the other side.
Remove from the pan and keep warm. Repeat with the
remaining dough.

Makes 12

Savoury scone crescent

*An attractive shaped loaf made from savoury scone mixture. Ideal
for a buffet. Make it on the day of serving.*

Butter or margarine 3 oz (75 g)
Small onion, finely chopped 1
100% wholemeal self-raising flour 1 lb (450 g)
Salt & pepper
Chopped fresh mixed herbs 2 tbsp (30 ml)
Egg, beaten 1
Milk ½ pt (300 ml)
Cheddar cheese, grated 6 oz (175 g)
Beaten egg to glaze
Sesame seeds to sprinkle

Preparation time: 25–30 minutes
Cooking time: 25–30 minutes

Melt 1 oz (25 g) of the butter in a small pan and add the
finely chopped onion. Cook gently until transparent. Cool.
Put the flour and 1 teaspoon of salt into a basin and rub in
the remaining butter until the mixture resembles fine crumbs.
Add the chopped fresh herbs and season generously with
pepper. Using a knife, stir in the beaten egg and enough

milk to give a soft but not sticky dough. Knead very lightly. Roll out the dough on a lightly floured surface to a rectangle approximately 16″ × 10″ (40 cm × 25 cm). Sprinkle the onion evenly over the dough to within 1″ (2.5 cm) of the edge. Then sprinkle with the cheese. Roll up like a swiss roll to form a long thin roll. Put on to a greased baking sheet and shape into a semicircle. Cut the dough at 1″ (2.5 cm) intervals to within 1″ (2.5 cm) of the inner edge. Brush with the lightly beaten egg and sprinkle with sesame seeds. Bake in the oven at 200°C (400°F/Mark 6) for 20–25 minutes or until golden and cooked through. Carefully transfer to a wire rack. Serve warm.

Makes 1 loaf

Sultana muffins

These are quick to make and are delicious served warm straight from the oven. Best served on day of making.

Butter or margarine 2 oz (50 g)
100% wholemeal self raising flour 6 oz (175 g)
Ground cinnamon 1 tsp (5 ml)
Raw brown sugar 1 oz (75 g)
Sultanas 3oz (75 g)
Egg, beaten 1
Milk 4 fl oz (100 ml)

Preparation time: 15 minutes
Cooking time: about 20 minutes

Rub the butter into the flour. Then stir in the cinnamon, sugar and sultanas. Mix the beaten egg and milk and stir into the dry ingredients using a knife. The mixture should be a stiff, dropping consistency. If it appears too stiff, add 1 or 2 tablespoons more milk. Drop rounded tablespoons of the mixture into well greased patty tins. Bake in the oven at

190°C (375°F/Mark 5) for about 20 minutes or until lightly browned. Remove the muffins from the tins and cool on a wire rack.

Alternative
Instead of sultanas add a similar amount of blueberries.

Makes 12

Potato soda bread

This quick bread goes well with chunky soups for lunch.

100% wholemeal self raising flour 1 lb (450 g)
Bicarbonate of soda 1 tsp (5 ml)
Salt 1 tsp (5 ml)
Butter or margarine 1 oz (25 g)
Potato, cooked & sieved 8 oz (225 g)
Egg, beaten 1
Milk, buttermilk or soya milk ½ pt (300 ml)

Preparation time: 25 minutes
Cooking time: 30–40 minutes

Combine the flour, bicarbonate of soda and salt in a large basin and rub in the butter. Add the sieved potato. Stir the beaten egg and the milk together and add to the dry ingredients. Mix to give a soft dough. Knead lightly on a floured surface, but be careful not to over-handle the mixture. Shape into an 8″ (20 cm) round and place on a greased baking tray. Cut a cross on top of the soda bread using a sharp knife. Bake in the oven at 200°C (400°F/Mark 6) for 30–40 minutes, or until the bread sounds hollow when tapped on the bottom. Cool on a wire tray. Serve fresh on the day of making.

Makes 1 loaf

Cakes &
Biscuits

Coconut fruit mince slice

This is a top favourite at Cranks.

Base
Butter or margarine 4 oz (100 g)
Raw brown sugar 2 oz (50 g)
100% self raising wholemeal flour 6 oz (175 g)

Topping
Eggs 2
Raw brown sugar 4 oz (100 g)
Vanilla essence 1 tsp (5 ml)
Fruit mince (*see page 177*) 8 oz (225 g)
Desiccated coconut 6 oz (175 g)
100% wholemeal flour 1 tbsp (15 ml)
Baking powder ½ tsp (2.5 ml)
Salt ¼ tsp (1.25 ml)

Preparation time: 25 minutes
Cooking time: 30–40 minutes

Cream the butter and sugar together until light and fluffy. Then stir in the flour and mix well. Press evenly over the base of a 7″ × 9″ (18 cm × 23 cm) cake tin, which has been lined with greased, greaseproof paper. Bake in the oven at 180°C (350°F/Mark 4) for approximately 10 minutes until pale golden brown.

Beat the eggs, sugar and vanilla until thick and creamy. Stir in the fruit mince and coconut and mix well. Then fold in the combined flour, baking powder and salt. Spread the topping evenly over the base. Return to the oven and bake for a further 20–30 minutes or until the fruit mince filling is set and golden. When cold cut into fingers.

Makes 16 slices

Carob meringue gâteau

Egg whites 6
Raw brown sugar 8 oz (225 g)
Carob powder 2 tbsp (30 ml)
Carob bar 3 oz (75 g)
Whipping cream ½ pt (300 ml)
Strawberries & carob curls (*see page 239*) to decorate

Preparation time: 45 minutes + cooling
Cooking time: 1–1¼ hours

Put the egg whites into a clean, dry bowl and whisk until soft peaks form. Gradually beat in the sugar, a tablespoon at a time. Then continue to beat until very thick and glossy. Using a metal spoon, carefully fold in the sifted carob powder. Divide the mixture between 2 round 8″ (20 cm) shallow tins which have been lined with greased non-stick silicone paper. Bake in the oven at 140°C (275°F/Mark 1) for about 1½ hours until crisp to the touch. Turn the oven off and leave the meringues to cool in the oven.

Put the broken carob bar into a bowl over gently simmering water. Stir until melted. Carefully stir in half the cream. Stir until combined then remove from the heat. Cool. Beat until lightly thickened.

Place a meringue round on a serving dish. Spread the carob mixture evenly over the meringue and cover with the second meringue layer. Lightly whip the remaining cream and spread over the top. Decorate with strawberries and carob curls.

Refrigerate for several hours before serving to soften the meringue.

Serves 8

Sponge fingers

These work very well with wholemeal flour.

Eggs 3
Raw brown sugar 3 oz (75 g)
Vanilla essence ¼ tsp (1.25 ml)
100% wholemeal flour 4 oz (100 g)
Salt, pinch
Carob bar (optional)

Preparation time: 20 minutes
Cooking time: 15–20 minutes

Put the eggs, sugar and vanilla into a basin over simmering water and beat until very thick and pale. Remove from the heat and carefully fold in the flour and salt. Spoon the mixture into a piping bag fitted with a medium-sized plain nozzle. Pipe finger lengths of the sponge mixture on to a greased baking tray, allowing room for them to spread. Bake in the oven at 190°C (375°F/Mark 5) for 5–7 minutes, until pale golden. Cool on a wire tray. If wished, dip both ends of the sponge fingers in melted carob bar.

Makes about 30–35

Strawberry cream sponge

This is a very light sponge cake suitable for a summer tea party and is best eaten on the day it is made.

Eggs 3
Raw brown sugar 2 oz (50 g)
Lemon, grated rind of ½
100% wholemeal flour 2 oz (50 g)
Arrowroot 1 oz (25 g)
Double or whipping cream, lightly whipped ½ pt (300 ml)
Raw sugar strawberry jam 6 tbsp (90 ml)
Strawberries to decorate (*see page 239*) 8 oz (225 g)

Preparation time: 30 minutes
Cooking time: about 25 minutes

Beat the eggs, sugar and lemon rind in a bowl or a food processor, until very thick and pale. Carefully fold in the flour and arrowroot. Spoon the mixture into an 8" (20 cm) round tin, which has been lined with greased, greaseproof paper. Bake in the oven at 180°C (350°F/Mark 4) for about 25 minutes until golden and firm to the touch. Turn out on to a wire tray to cool. Split the cake into two halves and sandwich with jam and half the cream. Decorate the top with the remaining whipped cream and fresh strawberries.

Victoria sponge

This 'classic' cake works beautifully with 100% wholemeal flour. The cake will keep for several days, but add the fresh cream filling on the day of serving.

Butter or margarine 4 oz (100 g)
Raw brown sugar 4 oz (100 g)
Vanilla essence ½ tsp (2.5 ml)
Eggs 3
100% self raising wholemeal flour 4 oz (100 g)
Raw sugar jam 4–6 tbsp (60–90 ml)
Double or whipping cream, lightly whipped ¼ pt (150 ml)
Ground almonds to decorate

Preparation time: 25 minutes
Cooking time: 25–30 minutes

Beat the butter, sugar and vanilla together until very light and fluffy. Add the eggs, one at a time, and beat well after each addition. Fold in the flour. Spoon into a greased, greaseproof paper-lined 8″ (20 cm) round tin and bake in the oven at 180°C (350°F/Mark 4) for 25–30 minutes, or until golden brown and firm to the touch. Cool on a wire tray. When cold, split the sponge and sandwich with jam and cream. Use a sieve to sprinkle ground almonds evenly over the top.

Yoghourt slice

We tested this recipe for a Loseley publicity leaflet and decided it was so delicious we'd keep it in our repertoire. It can also be served as a dessert.

Base
Digestive biscuits, crushed (see page 226) 6 oz (175 g)
Butter or margarine 3 oz (75 g)

Topping
Cottage cheese 1 lb (450 g)
Natural yoghourt 9.5 oz (270 g)
Vanilla essence 1 tsp (5 ml)
Lemon juice 1 tbsp (15 ml)
Honey 3 fl oz (75 ml)
Salt ¼ tsp (1.25 ml)
Full cream milk powder 1 tbsp (15 ml)
100% wholemeal flour 1 oz (25 g)
Eggs, separated 3
Sultanas 4 oz (100 g)

Preparation time: 25–30 minutes
Cooking time: 50–60 minutes

Mix the biscuit crumbs and melted butter together and press evenly over the base of an 8″ × 10″ (20 cm × 25 cm) cake tin lined with foil.

Put the cottage cheese through a fine sieve and add the yoghourt, vanilla, lemon juice, honey, salt, milk powder, flour and egg yolks. Beat until smooth. (Alternatively, put these ingredients into a food processor and beat until smooth. There is no need to sieve the cottage cheese.) Fold in the sultanas. Stiffly whisk the egg whites and fold into the mixture. Pour over the prepared base. Bake in the oven at 180°C (350°F/Mark 4) for 50–60 minutes until the filling is set and light golden brown. Cool in the tin. Then cut into squares. Serve just warm or cold.

Serves 6–8

Fudge brownies

These chewy brownies are a Cranks variation on the American favourite.

Eggs 3
Raw brown sugar 5 oz (150 g)
Salt ¼ tsp (1.25 ml)
Vanilla essence 1 tsp (5 ml)
Carob bars, chopped 6 oz (150 g)
Butter or margarine 4 oz (100 g)
100% wholemeal self raising flour 4 oz (100 g)
Sultanas 2 oz (50 g)
Shelled walnuts, chopped 1 oz (25 g)
Double cream 5 tbsp (75 ml)

Preparation time: about 30 minutes
Cooking time: about 30 minutes

Beat the eggs, sugar, salt and vanilla until light and frothy. Put 3 oz (75 g) chopped carob bar and the butter into a bowl and place over a pan of gently simmering water. Stir until melted and cool slightly. Then stir into the egg and sugar mixture. Using a metal spoon, fold in the flour, then add the sultanas and chopped walnuts and mix well. Pour into a greased, greaseproof paper-lined 8″ × 10″ (20 × 25 cm) cake tin. Bake in the oven at 180°C (350°F/Mark 4) for about 30 minutes, or until slightly firm to the touch. Cool in the tin.

Put the cream into a small pan and bring to the boil. Remove from the heat and stir in the remaining chopped carob bar. Stir until melted. Pour over the cake in the tin and smooth the top with a spatula or palette knife. When set cut into squares.

Makes 16

Fruit & nut cake

A firm fruit cake which keeps very well and looks most attractive with whole nuts and fruit baked on the top. Different fruits can be used, such as pears, peaches, mango or pineapple.

Stoned dates 8 oz (225 g)
Dried apricots 8 oz (225 g)
Dried figs 8 oz (225 g)
Whole blanched almonds 4 oz (100 g)
Brazil nuts, shelled 8 oz (225 g)
Eggs 3
Raw brown sugar 3 oz (75 g)
Raw sugar apricot jam 2 tbsp (30 ml)
Vanilla essence 1 tsp (5 ml)
Brandy 1 tbsp (15 ml)
Butter or margarine 3 oz (75 g)
100% wholemeal flour 3 oz (75 g)
Baking powder ½ tsp (2.5 ml)
Honey 1 tbsp (15 ml)

Preparation time: 30 minutes
Cooking time: about 1½ hours

Chop the fruit into fairly large pieces and leave the nuts whole. Mix together and put aside about half a cup of the fruit and nuts for decorating. Beat the eggs until light and fluffy. Then add the sugar, jam, vanilla and brandy and beat well. Gradually beat in the softened butter. Stir in the combined flour and baking powder and the fruit and nuts and mix well. Spoon the mixture into a greaseproof paper-lined 9″ × 5″ (23 cm × 12 cm) loaf tin. Place the reserved fruit and nuts on top, pressing gently down into the mixture. Bake in the oven at 150°C (300°F/Mark 2) for approximately 1½ hours, or until the cake is firm to the touch. Allow to cool in the tin for 10 minutes before turning out on to a wire tray. While still warm, brush the top of the cake with honey.

Cranks party cake

The perfect birthday cake. We find the orange flavour is very popular with children – coffee for more sophisticated adults. Just add the right number of candles!

Butter or margarine 6 oz (175 g)
Raw pale brown sugar 6 oz (175 g)
Large orange, grated rind & juice of 1
Eggs, separated 3
100% wholemeal self raising flour 6 oz (175 g)
Salt, pinch

Icing & decoration
Butter or margarine 4 oz (100 g)
Raw pale brown sugar 6 oz (175 g)
Large orange, grated rind & juice of 1
Toasted flaked almonds or chopped walnuts (*see page 20*)
   3 oz (75 g)

Preparation time: 45 minutes
Cooking time: 20 minutes

Grease and line the base of three 7″ (18 cm) sandwich tins. Cream the butter and sugar together until light and fluffy. Then beat in the orange rind and egg yolks. Fold in the flour and sufficient orange juice to give a soft dropping consistency. Whisk the egg whites with a pinch of salt until stiff. Then fold into the creamed mixture. Divide the sponge mixture between the prepared tins. Level the surface and bake in the oven at 180°C (350°F/Mark 4) for 15–20 minutes until risen and firm to the touch. Cool on a wire tray.

Icing & decoration
Cream the butter and sugar until really pale and fluffy. Beat in the orange rind and sufficient juice to give a soft spreading consistency.

Sandwich the cakes together with about one third of the icing. Use the remaining icing to cover the top and sides of the cake in a swirling pattern. Press the nuts into the sides of the cake.

Alternatives
Lemon Use 1 large lemon instead of the orange.

Coffee Replace the orange by adding 3 tablespoons cold strong black coffee to the cake mixture. To make coffee icing add sufficient cold strong black coffee to the butter and sugar mixture to give a soft spreading consistency.

Serves 12

Lemon madeira cake

To make this lovely lemony cake extra special top it with Raw sugar icing (see page 219) and decorate it with a sprinkling of lemon zest.

Butter or margarine 6 oz (175 g)
Raw brown sugar 6 oz (175 g)
Eggs 3
Lemons, grated rind and juice of 2
100% wholemeal flour 8 oz (225 g)
Baking powder 1½ tsp (7.5 ml)

Preparation time: 20 minutes
Cooking time: about 1¼ hours

Grease and line the base of a 2 lb (900 g) loaf tin. Cream the butter and sugar until pale and fluffy. Beat in the eggs, one at a time. Then stir in the grated lemon rind. If the mixture starts to curdle, beat in a little of the measured flour. Mix the flour and baking powder together and fold into the mixture. Stir in sufficient lemon juice to give a soft dropping consistency. Transfer the mixture to the prepared tin. Level the surface and make a slight dip in the centre. Bake at 170°C (325°F/Mark 3) for about 1¼ hours until risen and firm to the touch – when it is cooked a skewer inserted into the centre of the cake should come out clean. Leave the cake to cool slightly in the tin, then transfer it to a wire tray.

Boiled fruit cake

This is an easy cake to make. It is beautifully moist and will keep for up to a week wrapped in paper in a tin.

Currants 4 oz (100 g)
Raisins 4 oz (100 g)
Sultanas 8 oz (225 g)
Stoned dates, chopped 3 oz (75 g)
Dried apricots, chopped 3 oz (75 g)
Raw brown sugar 4 oz (100 g)
Orange juice 5 fl oz (150 ml)
Orange, grated rind of 1

Raw sugar apricot jam 4 oz (100 g)
Butter or margarine 8 oz (225 g)
Eggs, lightly beaten 3
Sherry or brandy 2 tbsp (30 ml)
100% wholemeal self raising flour 8 oz (225 g)
Ground mixed spice 1 tsp (5 ml)
Ground cinnamon 1 tsp (5 ml)
Ground ginger 1 tsp (5 ml)
Whole blanched almonds, split, to decorate
    1–2 oz (25–50 g)

Preparation time: 25 minutes
Cooking time: 1½–2 hours

Put the currants, raisins, sultanas, chopped dates, chopped dried apricots, sugar, orange juice, rind, jam and butter into a saucepan. Stir over the heat until the butter is melted. Bring to the boil and simmer gently, covered, for 1 minute. Remove from the heat. When the mixture is cold add the lightly beaten eggs and the brandy or sherry. Fold in the dry ingredients and mix together well. Grease and line an 8″ (20 cm) cake tin with a double thickness of greaseproof paper. Secure brown paper round the outside of the tin. Turn the mixture into the tin, smooth the top and decorate with the almonds. Bake in the oven at 150°C (300°F/Mark 2) for 1½–2 hours, or until a skewer inserted into the middle of the cake comes out clean. If the top browns too quickly, cover with brown paper. Cool in the tin. Transfer the cake to a wire tray and remove the paper.

Carob almond cake

This rich cake is best eaten freshly made and should not be refrigerated. It can also be served as a dessert.

Carob bar 4 oz (100 g)
Brandy 2 tbsp (30 ml)
Butter or margarine 4 oz (100 g)
Raw brown sugar 4 oz (100 g)
Eggs, separated 3
Ground almonds 1 oz (25 g)
Almond essence ¼ tsp (1.25 ml)
100% wholemeal self raising flour 1½ oz (40 g)
Double or whipping cream ¼ pt (150 ml)
Extra ground almonds to decorate 1 oz (25 g)

Preparation time: 40 minutes
Cooking time: about 25 minutes

Melt the broken carob bar together with the brandy over a saucepan of hot water. Cream the butter and sugar until light and fluffy. Gradually beat in the egg yolks. Then add the melted carob, almonds and the essence and mix well. Whisk the egg whites until soft peaks form. Using a metal spoon, fold in 2 tablespoons of the egg white to soften the mixture, then fold in the flour. Finally fold in the remaining egg white. Spoon the mixture into an 8″ (20 cm) round cake tin which has been lined with greased, greaseproof paper. Bake in the oven at 180°C (350°F/Mark 4) for approximately 25 minutes. Leave the cake to cool in the tin for 10 minutes. Then turn it out on to a wire tray.

When the cake is cold split it in half and, just before serving, fill with whipped cream. To decorate place 1″ (2.5 cm) strips of paper across the top of the cake, leaving a 1″ (2.5 cm) space in between each. Using a sieve, sprinkle the extra ground almonds over the top. Then carefully remove the paper strips leaving a striped effect.

Christmas cake

A rich fruit cake which improves with keeping. This recipe can also be used for a wedding, birthday or other celebration cake.

Raisins 2¼ lb (1 kg)
Currants 1 lb (450 g)
Stoned dates, chopped 6 oz (175 g)
Cooked prunes, stoned & chopped 4 oz (100 g)
Flaked almonds 8 oz (225 g)
Butter or margarine 14 oz (400 g)
Raw brown sugar 14 oz (400 g)
Eggs 8
Lemon, grated rind of 1
Orange, grated rind of 1
Black treacle 1 tbsp (15 ml)
100% wholemeal flour 1 lb (450 g)
Salt 1 tsp (5 ml)
Ground nutmeg, allspice, cinnamon & ginger 1 tsp (5 ml)
  of each
Sherry 5 tbsp (75 ml)

Preparation time: 40 minutes + leaving overnight
Cooking time: 5 hours

Grease and line a cake tin with a double thickness of grease-proof paper. Secure brown paper round the outside of the tin. Combine the raisins, currants, dates, prunes and almonds in a large basin. Cream the butter and sugar until pale and fluffy, then beat in the eggs one at a time. Stir in the lemon and orange rind and the black treacle. If there is any sign of curdling, stir in a spoonful of flour. Combine the flour, salt and spices and fold into the mixture alternately with the mixed fruits. Stir in the sherry. Turn the mixture into the prepared tin. Smooth the surface and bake in the oven at 150°C (300°F/Mark 2) for 1 hour. Reduce heat to 140°C (275°F/Mark 1) for a further 4 hours. Cover with greaseproof paper if the surface is overbrowning. Leave the cake to cool in the tin overnight, then turn it out and wrap it in a double thickness of kitchen foil. Store in a cool dry place until required.

To decorate

Cover with 2 lb (900 g) almond paste or mock marzipan and icing (*see following three recipes*).

Makes 10" (25 cm) round or 9" (23 cm) square cake

Almond paste

Ground almonds 4 oz (100 g)
Raw pale brown sugar 4 oz (100 g)
Beaten egg 2 tbsp (30 ml)
Almond essence ½ tsp (2.5 ml)

Preparation time: 10 minutes

Sift the ground almonds and sugar into a basin. Stir together the egg and almond essence and mix with the almonds to form a soft, manageable 'dough'.

Makes about ½ lb (225 g)

Mock marzipan

An alternative to almond paste for vegans.

Raw pale brown sugar 10 oz (300 g)
Soya flour 4 oz (100 g)
Margarine, softened 2 oz (50 g)
Almond essence 1 tsp (5 ml)
Water 1–2 tbsp (15–30 ml)

Preparation time: 10 minutes

Mix the dry ingredients together in a basin and rub in the margarine. Add the almond essence and sufficient water to mix to a soft, manageable 'dough'.

Makes about 1 lb (450 g)

Raw sugar icing

Raw pale brown sugar 4 oz (100 g)
Lemon juice 1–2 tbsp (15–30 ml)
Vanilla essence, few drops

Preparation time: 10 minutes

Mill the sugar in a coffee grinder or pass it through a fine sieve. Add the vanilla essence and enough lemon juice to give a spreading consistency when beaten well. Use to coat biscuits or the top of a cake.

Honey snaps

These crisp, rolled biscuits are perfect with afternoon tea. Don't fill them until just before serving.

Butter or margarine 2 oz (50 g)
Raw demerara sugar 2 oz (50 g)
Honey 2 oz (50 g)
100% wholemeal flour 2 oz (50 g)
Salt, pinch
Ground ginger ½ tsp (2.5 ml)
Lemon juice ½ tsp (2.5 ml)
Whipped cream or Greek yoghourt to fill ¼ pt (150 ml)

Preparation time: 30 minutes
Cooking time: about 25 minutes

Put the butter, sugar and honey into a saucepan and stir over the heat until the butter has melted. Remove from the heat and mix in the flour, salt and ginger. Then stir in the lemon juice.

Place teaspoonfuls of the mixture on to a well greased baking tray, allowing room for the biscuits to spread. Flatten out well with the back of an oiled teaspoon. It is best to make only 3 or 4 at a time as once the biscuits are cooked they become brittle very quickly and are difficult to roll. Bake in the oven at 160°C (325°F/Mark 3) for approximately 8 minutes or until golden brown.

Leave the biscuits to cool for about a minute, then carefully loosen them with a palette knife. Roll immediately around the handle of a wooden spoon, keeping the top of the biscuit to the outside, and allow to go cold and firm. Place on a wire tray. Just before serving pipe whipped cream or a little thick Greek yoghourt into the end of each honey snap.

Makes about 24

Orange wafer biscuits

Try these – they are well worth the effort! Serve them with Loseley ice creams or fresh fruit salad.

Egg white 1
Raw brown sugar 2 oz (50 g)
Butter or margarine 1 oz (25 g)
100% wholemeal flour 1 oz (25 g)
Orange, grated rind of 1

Preparation time: 20 minutes
Cooking time: about 25 minutes

Whisk the egg white in a small basin until stiff. Gradually whisk in the sugar. Stir in the melted butter, alternately with the flour. Then fold in the orange rind.

Drop teaspoonfuls of the mixture on to a greased oven tray allowing room for them to spread. Flatten the mixture out very thinly. Bake in the oven at 190°C (375°F/Mark 5) for 5–6 minutes or until pale golden. Loosen the biscuits using a spatula. Then, while they are still hot, curl them over a lightly greased rolling pin and leave to go cold. Only make 3 biscuits at a time as they harden very quickly. When cold store in an airtight container, or freeze.

Makes about 15

Carob fruit & nut squares

We serve these with after dinner coffee in our 'Dine and Wine' restaurant.

Carob bar, chopped 12 oz (350 g)
Sultanas 4 oz (100 g)
Shredded coconut, toasted (*see page 20*) 2 oz (50 g)
Brazil nuts, chopped 2 oz (50 g)
Brandy or sherry 1 tbsp (15 ml)
Double cream 3 tbsp (45 ml)

Preparation time: 15–20 minutes + chilling
No cooking required

Put the chopped carob into a basin over simmering water. Stir until melted, being careful not to overheat the carob. Remove from the heat and stir in the sultanas, coconut and the chopped brazil nuts. Then stir in the brandy and cream. Spread the mixture evenly over the base of an 8″ (20 cm) square tin lined with foil. Refrigerate until firm. Cut into small squares.

Makes about 50

Honey nut bars

An after dinner delight. A homemade, healthful alternative to a box of chocolates!

Thin honey 12 oz (350 g)
Butter or margarine 4 oz (100 g)
Shelled hazelnuts, toasted 4 oz (100 g)
Shredded coconut, toasted 4 oz (100 g)
Flaked almonds, toasted 4 oz (100 g)
Sesame seeds, toasted 2 oz (50 g) (*see page 20*)

Preparation time: 15–20 minutes + cooling
Cooking time: 20 minutes

Put the honey and the butter into a medium-sized saucepan. Stir over a low heat until the butter has melted. Bring to the boil. Then simmer gently for 10 minutes or until the honey mixture is a pale golden brown. Remove from the heat and carefully stir in the hazelnuts, coconut, almonds and sesame seeds. Spread the mixture evenly over the base of a greased 8″ × 10″ (20 cm × 25 cm) cake tin. Cool. Then refrigerate until firm. Cut into tiny bars.

Makes about 60

Honey & sesame seed squares

These are easy and quick to make and a favourite with children.

Sesame seeds 2 oz (50 g)
Jumbo oats 4 oz (100 g)
Honey 3 oz (75 g)
Sunflower oil 4 tbsp (60 ml)
Sultanas 2 oz (50 g)
Raw brown sugar 1 oz (25 g)

Preparation time: 10 minutes
Cooking time: 30–35 minutes

Mix all the ingredients together well and press into a greased 8″ (20 cm) shallow square tin. Bake at 180°C (350°F/Mark 4) for 30–35 minutes until golden brown. Cool in the tin, then cut into squares. Transfer to a wire tray and leave to go cold. Store in an airtight container, or freeze.

Makes 9

Coconut oat bars

Rolled oats 3 oz (75 g)
Sultanas 4 oz (100 g)
100% wholemeal self raising flour 2 oz (50 g)
Raw brown sugar 2 oz (50 g)
Shredded coconut 2 oz (50 g)
Butter or margarine 5 oz (150 g)
Honey 1 tbsp (15 ml)

Preparation time: 15 minutes
Cooking time: 15–20 minutes

Combine the oats, sultanas, flour, sugar and coconut in a bowl. Melt the butter and honey together and stir into the dry ingredients. Mix well. Press the mixture over the base of a well greased 8″ × 10″ (20 × 25 cm) cake tin. Bake in the oven at 180°C (350°F/Mark 4) for 15–20 minutes, or until pale golden. Cut into bars while still hot and leave to cool in the tin. Store in an airtight container, or freeze.

Makes about 18

Hazelnut fingers

Butter or margarine 8 oz (225 g)
Raw brown sugar 2 oz (50 g)
Vanilla essence ½ tsp (2.5 ml)

**Shelled hazelnuts, roasted & ground (*see page 20*)
  2 oz (50 g)**
100% wholemeal self raising flour 8 oz (225 g)
Salt, pinch
Carob bar, chopped (optional) 6 oz (175 g)

Preparation time: 25 minutes
Cooking time: 20–30 minutes

Cream the butter, sugar and vanilla together until light and fluffy. Stir in the hazelnuts, flour and salt and mix until combined. Put the mixture into a piping bag fitted with a large star nozzle. Pipe finger lengths of the mixture on to greased oven trays. Bake in the oven at 190°C (350°F/Mark 4) for 10–15 minutes until pale golden. Cool on the trays.

Melt the chopped carob over hot water and dip each end of the biscuits into the carob. Place on a wire rack until set. Store in an airtight container, or freeze.

Makes about 40

Hazelnut carob biscuits

Butter or margarine 6 oz (175 g)
Raw brown sugar 3 oz (75 g)
Egg 1
Vanilla essence ½ tsp (2.5 ml)
100% wholemeal self raising flour 8 oz (225 g)
Hazelnuts, roasted & chopped (*see page 20*) 4 oz (100 g)
Carob bar, chopped 3 oz (75 g)
Extra carob bar, chopped (optional) 3 oz (75 g)

Preparation time: 30 minutes
Cooking time: 12–15 minutes

Cream the butter and sugar together until light and fluffy. Add the egg and vanilla and beat until well combined. Stir in the flour, then add the chopped hazelnuts and chopped carob bar. Mix well. Roll dessertspoonfuls of the mixture into balls. Place them on lightly greased baking trays, allowing room to spread, and flatten with a fork. Bake in the oven at 180°C (350°F/Mark 4) for 12–15 minutes until golden brown. Cool slightly on the trays before transferring the biscuits to a wire rack to cool completely.

Put the extra chopped carob into a small bowl and stir over hot water until it melts. Spoon the carob into the corner of a small greaseproof paper piping bag. Snip off the corner and run the carob decoratively over each biscuit. Allow to set. Store in an airtight container, or freeze.

Makes about 18

Muesli biscuits

Dry muesli 8 oz (225 g)
Raw brown sugar 2 oz (50 g)
100% wholemeal flour 4 oz (100 g)
Ground almonds 3 oz (75 g)
Butter or margarine 6 oz (175 g)
Honey 3 tbsp (45 ml)
Bicarbonate of soda ½ tsp (2.5 ml)

Preparation time: 25 minutes
Cooking time: 10–15 minutes

Combine the muesli, sugar, flour and ground almonds. Melt the butter and honey in a small saucepan. Remove from the heat and stir in the bicarbonate of soda. Add this mixture to the dry ingredients and mix well. Place rounded dessertspoonfuls of the mixture on to greased oven trays and flatten with a fork. Bake in the oven at 190°C (375°F/Mark 5) for 10–15 minutes, or until golden. Cool on a wire tray. Store in an airtight container, or freeze.

Makes about 24

Coconut oatmeal cookies

Butter or margarine 4 oz (100 g)
Raw brown sugar 4 oz (100 g)
Egg 1
Vanilla essence 1 tsp (5 ml)
Porridge oats 4 oz (100 g)
Desiccated coconut 3 oz (75 g)
Mixed nuts, chopped 2 oz (50 g)

Preparation time: 20 minutes
Cooking time: 10–15 minutes

Cream the butter and sugar together until pale and fluffy and
then beat in the egg and vanilla. Stir in the oats, coconut and
nuts. Divide the mixture into 15 even-sized balls. Place on a
lightly greased baking tray allowing room for them to spread.
Flatten well with a fork. Bake in the oven at 180°C (350°F/
Mark 4) for approximately 10 minutes until golden. Cool
slightly before transferring to a wire tray. Store in an airtight
container, or freeze.

Makes 15

Digestive biscuits

*Good as plain biscuits, or with cheese. They can also be crushed
with a rolling pin and used with melted butter as a crumb base.*

100% wholemeal flour 6 oz (175 g)
Medium oatmeal 1½ oz (40 g)
Baking powder 1 tsp (5 ml)
Salt ½ tsp (2.5 ml)
Butter or margarine 3 oz (75 g)
Raw brown sugar 2 oz (50 g)
Milk or soya milk to mix 3 tbsp (45 ml)

Preparation time: about 30 minutes
Cooking time: 20–25 minutes

Mix all the dry ingredients, except the sugar, together. Rub in the butter until the mixture resembles fine crumbs, stir in the sugar and add the milk. Stir well until the dough is firm but manageable. Roll out fairly thinly on a lightly floured board and stamp out 3″ (7.5 cm) rounds. Place on a greased baking sheet and bake in the oven at 180°C (350°F/Mark 4) for 20–25 minutes, until light brown. Cool on a wire tray and store in an airtight tin.

Makes about 18

Drinks

Pineapple coconut crush

A deliciously refreshing summer drink.

Creamed coconut 4 oz (100 g)
Boiling water ½ pt (300 ml)
Large pineapple ½
Ice
Pineapple Juice ½ pt (300 ml)
Mint leaves & fresh pineapple pieces to decorate

Preparation time: 20 minutes

Mix the coconut with the boiling water and stir together well.
Cool. Peel the pineapple and, if necessary, remove the centre
if it is tough. Chop roughly and put into a liquidizer or food
processor. Blend until smooth. Add some ice, the coconut
mixture and pineapple juice and blend until frothy. Pour into
glasses and decorate with pineapple pieces and mint leaves.

Makes about 2 pints (just over 1 litre)

White wine cup

Raspberries or strawberries, sliced 2 oz (50 g)
Large ripe peach, stone removed & sliced 1
Pale brown raw sugar 2 tbsp (30 ml)
Fresh mint leaves, sliced across 12

Dry or medium dry white wine, chilled, 1 bottle
Soda water, chilled, 17½ fl oz (500 ml)
Crushed ice

Preparation time: 15 minutes + 30 minutes standing time

Put the raspberries, peach, sugar and sliced mint leaves in a jug or large bowl. Leave for about half an hour until the juice begins to run from the fruit. Then pour in the white wine and soda water. Stir in the crushed ice.

Makes 6–8 glasses

Mixed fruit cup

Oranges, juice of 4
Grapefruit, juice of 3
Red grape juice ½ pt (300 ml)
Ice
Mint leaves or fresh basil
Prepared fresh fruit (kiwi fruit, strawberries, lemon slices, raspberries, grapes)
Sparkling mineral water, chilled ½ pt (300 ml)

Preparation time: 20 minutes

Mix the fruit juices with some ice and mint leaves, or basil, in a glass bowl. Add the fresh fruit. Refrigerate and stir in the chilled mineral water just before serving. Serve very cold.

Makes about 2 pints (just over 1 litre)

Luaka tea punch

We recommend Luaka, a low tannin tea, for this but any delicately flavoured tea may be used. Be careful not to leave it to infuse for too long as it spoils the flavour.

Boiling water 2 pts (1.2 l)
Luaka tea 6 tsp (30 ml)
Honey to taste
Oranges, juice of 6
Ice
Lemon, or lime, slices 6
Mint leaves to taste

Preparation time: about 20 minutes

Pour the boiling water on to the tea leaves and leave to infuse for not more than 5 minutes. Strain. Sweeten to taste with honey. Stir in the orange juice, ice, lemon slices and mint leaves. Serve well chilled.

Makes 3 pints (about 2 litres)

Mulled wine

A favourite winter party drink.

Red wine 1 bottle
Brandy 2 tbsp (30 ml)
Oranges, juice of 2
Honey 2 tbsp (30 ml)
Cinnamon sticks 2
Whole cloves 15
Whole nutmeg, finely grated ¼
Orange, sliced 1
Lemon, sliced 1

Preparation time: 15 minutes
Cooking time: 10 minutes

Put all the ingredients into a saucepan. Heat very gently, but do not allow to boil. Serve hot.

Makes about 1½ pints (just under 1 litre)

Cider punch

We recommend using Aspall cider and apple juice made from unsprayed apples for this.

Cider 1¾ pt (1 l)
Apple juice 1 pt (600 ml)
Ice
Lemon 1

Preparation time: 10 minutes

Put the cider, apple juice and some ice into a large bowl or large glass jug. Thinly slice the lemon and add it to the punch. Refrigerate until ready to serve.

Makes about 3 pints (1¾ litres)

Cranks homemade lemonade

Thin-skinned lemons 4
Raw brown sugar 6 oz (175 g)
Boiling water 1½ pts (900 ml)

Preparation time: 20 minutes

Scrub the lemons, halve them, then squeeze out the juice and pulp in a large jug or bowl with the sugar and pour ½ pint (300 ml) boiling water over. Stir until the sugar dissolves. Add the lemon halves and another pint (600 ml) boiling water. Stir well, then cover and leave to cool. Strain, squeezing out the juice from the lemon halves, and serve.

Alternative
Honeyed lemonade Instead of the sugar use 3 oz (75 g) of honey, or more to taste.

Makes about 1½ pints (900 ml)

Tomato juice cocktail

This refreshing drink can be served as a first course.

Tomato juice 1¾ pts (1 l)
Soya sauce 1 tbsp (15 ml)
Ice
Salt & pepper to taste
Cayenne pepper to taste
Lemon, sliced 1
Cucumber ½

Preparation time: 15 minutes

Put the tomato juice, soya sauce, some ice, salt, pepper, cayenne and lemon slices into a jug. Mix well. Pour into glasses. Cut cucumber sticks slightly taller than the glasses. Serve with a cucumber swivel stick in each glass.

Makes about 2 pints (just over 1 litre)

Strawberry orange blush

Use ripe, really red strawberries to ensure a good flavour.

Ripe strawberries 8 oz (225 g)
Oranges, juice of 2
Ice

Preparation time: 10 minutes

Wash and hull the strawberries, and put them together with the orange juice and some ice into a liquidizer goblet. Blend until smooth and pour into long stemmed glasses.

Serves 4

Yoghourt, milk & fruit drink

Prepared fruit (raspberries, apricots, strawberries)
  4 oz (100 g)
Natural yoghourt ¼ pt (150 ml)
Milk ½ pt (300 ml)
Raw brown sugar or honey

Preparation time: 5 minutes

Put the fresh fruit, yoghourt and milk into a liquidizer goblet.
Add the sugar or honey to taste and blend until smooth.
Sieve, if wished, before serving.

Serves 2–3

Sparkling fruit drinks

*Concentrated unsweetened fruit juices are refreshing diluted with
natural sparkling mineral water. Ideal for children's parties.*

Take any flavour (orange, grapefruit, strawberry, raspberry)
of unsweetened concentrated fruit juice and make up to taste
with sparkling mineral water. Whisk with a small balloon
whisk and serve.

Garnishes

Fresh herbs One of the prettiest and most natural garnishes are sprigs of fresh herbs or finely chopped herbs. Choose from parsley, coriander, chives, tarragon, basil, mint, bay, borage flowers etc.

Vegetable circles Place circles of thinly sliced vegetables on top of each other so the coloured edges show. Try a slice of beetroot, topped with cucumber and then a slice of radish. Or a circle of cucumber or courgette covered with a slice of carrot and a circle of spring onion. Add a squeeze of lemon to prevent discolouration. Slices of tomato look attractive with just a sprig of parsley in the centre.

Spring onion garnish Trim the spring onions then slice them diagonally very thinly. Cover with cold water until ready for use. Drain thoroughly and use to sprinkle over savouries.

Spring onion curls Trim the ends of the spring onions. Using scissors, or a small sharp knife, cut along the length of the onions in thin strips, leaving about ½" (1 cm) at the base uncut. Put into a bowl of iced water for several hours until they curl into palm tree shapes.

Tomato flowers Using a small sharp knife, make continuous zigzag cuts through the centre of a tomato so that they meet in the centre. Open out into 2 halves.

Radish flowers Large trimmed radishes can be cut in the same way as tomato flowers. Or trim the radishes and using a small sharp knife cut thin slices almost through the radish. Soak in iced water for several hours until they open out.

Cucumber slices Using a small sharp knife, cut grooves of skin away down the length of the cucumber. Cut into slices. This gives them an attractive serrated edge.

Pepper rings Cut through small, different coloured peppers to make attractive rings.

Decorations

Strawberry fans Wash the strawberries but do not hull them. Make a cut in the centre of the strawberries from the pointed end to the stem but do not cut right through. Spread them out in a fan shape. Use to decorate strawberry mousses, sponges and trifles.

Lemon, lime and orange twists Slice the lemon, lime or orange thinly. Make one cut from the centre to the outside edge of each slice. Twist the cut edges in opposite directions so that the slices will stand up.

Carob rose leaves Put a chopped 3 oz (75 g) carob bar into a small bowl and place it over a pan of gently simmering water. Stir until melted. Be careful not to overheat the carob. Choose some rose leaves, wipe them with a damp cloth and pat dry. Using a small spatula or knife, or artist's paint brush, spread the carob evenly over the underside of the leaf. Make sure the carob does not run over the edges as this will make it difficult to remove the leaf. Use the stem as a handle to hold the leaf. Carefully place the leaves on a tray lined with foil or non-stick paper. Refrigerate until the carob has set. Then carefully peel the leaf from the carob. These make pretty decorations for cakes, desserts and ice creams. They can be stored in a rigid container in the fridge, or will freeze for several weeks.

Carob curls Leave the carob bar at room temperature. Then using a swivel potato peeler, peel off carob curls. Useful for decorating cakes and desserts. They can be stored in a rigid container in the fridge or freezer for several weeks.

Piping Whipped cream, thick set yoghourt, mayonnaise, meringue, some biscuit mixtures and puréed vegetables may all be piped to give a decorative effect. Use a plain or star nozzle in a nylon or cotton piping bag. Squeeze the end to exclude air. Pipe shell shapes, straight lines, or rosettes with a star nozzle, and dots or straight lines with a plain nozzle.

Index

Index

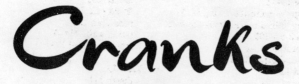

BRANCHES

CRANKS MARSHALL STREET
8 Marshall Street, London W1
0171-437 9431

⊖Oxford Circus
Open Mon-Tues-Fri 8am to 8pm
Wed-Thurs 8am to 9pm
Saturday 9am to 9pm

CRANKS TOTTENHAM STREET
9-11 Tottenham Street, London W1
0171-631 3912

⊖Goodge Street
Open Mon-Fri 8am to 7.30pm
Saturday 9am to 7.30pm
Shop Mon-Fri 8am to 6.30pm

CRANKS LEICESTER SQUARE
17-19 Great Newport St, London WC2
0171-836 5226

⊖Leicester Square
Open Mon-Fri 8am to 10pm
Saturday 10am to 10pm
Sunday 12 noon to 9pm

CRANKS CANARY WHARF
Concourse Level, 15 Cabot Place,
London E14
0171-513 0678

⊖Canary Wharf
Open Mon-Fri 7.30am to 6pm

CRANKS ST. CHRISTOPHER'S PLACE
23 Barrett Street, London W1
0171-495 1340

⊖Bond Street
Open Mon-Fri 8am to 7.30pm
Saturday 9am to 7pm

CRANKS CHARING CROSS
8 Adelaide Street, London WC2
0171-836 0660

⊖Charing Cross
Open Mon-Fri 8am to 8pm
Saturday 9am to 7pm
Sunday 12 noon to 6pm

CRANKS WEST COUNTRY
The Cider Press Centre
Dartington, Devon
01803-862 388

M4, M5, A38
Open Mon-Sat 10am to 5pm
Sundays during Summer

Cranks, Eardley House, 182-184 Campden Hill Road, London W8 7AS

All Orion/Phoenix titles are available at your local bookshop or
from the following address:

Littlehampton Book Services
Cash Sales Department L
14 Eldon Way, Lineside Industrial Estate
Littlehampton
West Sussex BN17 7HE

telephone 01903 721596, *facsimile* 01903 730914

Payment can either be made by credit card (Visa and Mastercard
accepted) or by sending a cheque or postal order made payable to
Littlehampton Book Services.
DO NOT SEND CASH OR CURRENCY.

Please add the following to cover postage and packing

UK and BFPO:
£1.50 for the first book, and 50P for each additional book to a
maximum of £3.50

Overseas and Eire:
£2.50 for the first book plus £1.00 for the second book and 50p
for each additional book ordered

BLOCK CAPITALS PLEASE

name of cardholder ....   *delivery address*
....   *(if different from cardholder)*
address of cardholder ....

postcode ....   *postcode* ....

☐ I enclose my remittance for £...............................

☐ please debit my Mastercard/Visa (delete as appropriate)

card number   □□□□□□□□□□□□□□□□□

expiry date   □□□□

signature ....

prices and availability are subject to change without notice